The Narrow Gate

Recalibration on the Spiritual Journey

A Retreat

2022

Edward Kleinguetl

outskirts press

Open to me the gate of holiness: I will enter and give thanks.
This is the Lord's own gate where the just may enter.
I will thank you for you have answered and are my savior.

—Psalm 118:19-21

Strive to enter through the narrow door, for many, I tell you,
will attempt to enter but will not be strong enough.

—Luke 13:24

Do not give your heart to that which does not satisfy your heart.

—Abba Poemen

Without repentance there is no cleansing from sin and without
cleansing from sin one cannot enter the Kingdom of Heaven.

—Patriarch Daniel of Romania

For Donna Rueby
and other lay leaders and clergy
who are passionately committed to the evangelization
and salvation of our young people,
combating secularization
and passing on the Deposit of Faith

Table of Contents

The Way

"Thomas said to him, 'Master, we do not know where you are going; how can we know the way?' Jesus said to him, 'I am the way and the truth and the life. No one comes to the Father except through me.'"
(John 14:5-6)

"There are two ways: one of life and one of death—
and there is a big difference between the two." [1]
(The Didache 1:1)

"Woe to the soul that does not have Christ dwelling in it; deserted and foul with the filth of the passions, it becomes a haven for all the vices." [2]
(St. Macarius the Great)

Opening Retreat Prayer

Glory to you, Christ our God, glory to you!

Heavenly King, Comforter, Spirit of Truth, everywhere present and filling all things, Treasury of Blessings and Giver of Life, come and dwell within us, cleanse us of all stain, and save our souls, O Gracious One.

Lord, Jesus Christ, open our hearts and minds to hear your voice. Speak tenderly to those who call upon your name. Speak, Lord, your servants are listening.

---

1 *The Didache: The Teaching of the Twelve Apostles,* trans. R. Joseph Owles (North Charleston, SC: CreateSpace, 2014), 1. The Didache is an important historical document of the Early Church, written in the first century.
2 St. Macarius, "Homily 28," in *The Liturgy of the Hours* (New York, NY: Catholic Book Publishing Corp., 1975), 596.

Opening Gospel Reading: The Narrow Gate

Matt. 7:13-21

A reading from the Holy Gospel according to St. Matthew.

Jesus said: "Enter through the narrow gate; for the gate is wide and the road broad that leads to destruction, and those who enter through it are many.

"How narrow the gate and constricted the road that leads to life. And those who find it are few.

"Beware of false prophets, who come to you in sheep's clothing, but underneath are ravenous wolves. By their fruits you will know them. Do people pick grapes from thorn-bushes, or figs from thistles? Just so, every good tree bears good fruit, and a rotten tree bears bad fruit. A good tree cannot bear bad fruit, nor can a rotten tree bear good fruit. Every tree that does not bear good fruit will be cut down and thrown into the fire. So by their fruits you will know them.

"Not everyone who says to me, 'Lord, Lord,' will enter the kingdom of heaven, but only the one who does the will of my Father in heaven."

The Gospel of the Lord.

Determining Priorities

Let us begin with two questions. First: What do I truly desire in life? Consider the evidence: What do I prioritize? Where do I spend my time? With whom do I associate? What is my North Star that drives me day-in and day-out? When we examine our lives, we will recognize what we truly desire in this life. As Christians, we need to consider whether our divinely intended purpose—internal blessedness with God in the life to come—is a priority and where it fits with everything else in our lives.

Second: Is my faith important to me? Consider, again, the evidence: Where does my faith fit among my priorities? How much time do I dedicate to it? Do I give my divinely created purpose much thought daily? Have I drifted from the path, maybe too far to the right or to the left? Is there a fire in my heart for Jesus Christ? Or, has my heart grown cold? Am I simply going through the motions?

We often find ourselves in the midst of a turbulent whirlpool within the secular world. We doubt. We question. We wonder where God is. Didn't Jesus promise us the abundant life?[3] If so, why can't we find it? Amid such confusion, emptiness and despair will often take root. We find ourselves wondering, "There has to be more …."

All of us are called to holiness, which is the life God intended for each of us. Periodically, it is important to recalibrate on the spiritual journey—to see where we are and determine the direction we intend to go. It is easy to become distracted or bogged down by the offers of the secular world, many of which, at least on the surface, seem far more enticing than a life of Christian virtue or the Way of the Cross. The glitz and attractive packaging seem so appealing that we often find ourselves drawn to them. The Devil has a great marketing team; he knows that we want quick fixes and an easier path in a society of convenience, instant access to information, and immediate gratification. We become less patient, resist struggles or inconveniences, and increasingly focus on ourselves.

Throughout this retreat, we will come back to these two questions

---

3   See John 10:10. All biblical quotes contained herein are from the NABRE 2011, unless otherwise specified.

about priorities—our desires and the importance of faith—to triangulate our position and determine the path forward. For now, we will assume that as participants, we are interested in salvation or at least open to the possibility.

Salvation

Even the word—*salvation*—has become distorted by secular culture. Simply put, salvation coincides with the final words of the Creed: "Life of the world to come." It is not this life, even in its most perfect state. We are on a journey preparing for true Paradise, which is not here. St. Thomas Aquinas provides us with three attributes of this life to come. First, in eternal life, man is united with God.[4] God himself is the reward, and as Jesus said in the Beatitudes, "Blessed are the clean of heart, for they shall see God."[5] When will this take place? St. John tells us: "Beloved, we are God's children now; what we shall be has not yet been revealed. We do know that when it is revealed we shall be like him, for we shall see him as he is."[6] By virtue of our Baptism, we are claimed as children of God and when the life to come is revealed, "we shall see him as he is."

Second, eternal life consists of perfect praise.[7] We will be filled with inexhaustible joy and happiness. Third, eternal life is the complete satisfaction of all our desires, a superabundance of which we are given more than we could ever hope for. St. Thomas writes, "The reason is that in this life no one can fulfill his longing, nor can any creature satisfy man's desire. Only God satisfies; he infinitely exceeds all other pleasures. That is why man can rest in nothing but God ...."[8]

---

4   Cf. St. Thomas Aquinas, "Conference," in *The Liturgy of the Hours*, vol. 4 (New York, NY: Catholic Book Publishing Corp., 1975), 563-4.
5   Matt. 5:8.
6   1 John 3:2.
7   Aquinas, 564.
8   Ibid.

This is eternal life described by Jesus and recorded in Sacred Scripture. So, what in this life can compare with an offer of superabundance? The short answer is: nothing, because every time we try to find something other than God to fill our longing, we generally come up empty.[9] Why do people not prioritize this amazing offer? There are likely myriad answers. One is that this life is not attainable in an instant. Perseverance is required, and some grow weary from the effort required, concluding it's just too hard and there are more attractive offers of the world that require less effort. Another reason that Jesus has defined discipleship as taking up one's cross.[10] For many, this is where Christianity hits a speedbump—who wants a simple inconvenience, much less a cross? With this, more appealing alternatives are sought. There has to be an easier way. However, the reality remains unchanged. Only God can satisfy the longing in every human heart—after all, he created that longing so that he could fill it. By the fact we are created in the divine image,[11] we were designed to be filled by his overwhelming love. One cannot fill infinite longing with finite things. Many have tried, yet the result is always the same: we come up empty. The proverbial definition of insanity is doing the same thing over and over again, expecting different results. Accordingly, we must try something different. If something other than God is not producing the result we want, perhaps it is time to reconsider God's offer of salvation.

Rediscovering the Way

Throughout Sacred Scripture, there is a continued differentiation between two distinct ways: one with God and one without. Jesus, in our opening reading, described the two ways as the narrow gate, which

---

9   See C.S. Lewis, *Mere Christianity* (New York: Macmillan, 1952), 53. "All that we call human history ... [is] the long, terrible story of man trying to find something other than God which will make him happy."
10   See Luke 9:23. "If anyone wishes to come after me, he must deny himself and take up his cross daily and follow me."
11   Cf. Gen. 1:27.

few will find and leads to eternal life, and the wide road leading to destruction. There are only two ways: with or without God. We have the freedom to choose, and God will respect our choice. There are distortions to these alternatives, with some desiring the way "with God, but not completely," as if there is a compromise. Do not be deceived! There is no middle way. When the rich young man walked away after Jesus detailed the requirements for eternal life,[12] Jesus did not run after him and say, "Wait! Perhaps we can make the requirements easier ...." On the contrary, Jesus respected his decision to walk away. Further, an all-in, immediate response is required. Jesus said elsewhere, "No one who sets a hand to the plow and looks to what was left behind is fit for the kingdom of God."[13]

St. Gregory Palamas identifies three points on the spiritual journey. The starting point is the grace received in Baptism. The end point is the perfection that will result at the Resurrection of the Dead, that for which we hope. The third is the stage between these two points, which St. Gregory calls the intermediate stage, life according to Christ's gospel "by which the God-fearing person is nourished, grows and is renewed, making progress day by day in the knowledge of God, righteousness, and sanctification."[14] By following this intermediate stage, a person "gradually reduces and cuts away his eagerness for things below, and transfers his longing from what is visible; physical and temporary to what is invisible, spiritual, and eternal."[15] We begin to realize nothing created for or of this world will ever provide the satisfaction we seek, and we begin to look to the other-worldly (the life to come).

That intermediate stage, the "everything else" between the two points, is where we want to focus during this retreat. If our hearts have lost their baptismal zeal, if they are not on fire with love for Jesus, if we feel lost or abandoned like sheep without a shepherd, if

---

12   See Mark 10:17-22.
13   Luke 9:62.
14   *Saint Gregory Palamas: The Homilies*, ed. and trans. Christopher Veniamin (Dalton, PA: Mount Thabor Publishing, 2016), 130. Homily Sixteen, no. 34.
15   Ibid.

we are filled with doubts or despair as if tossed about in a turbulent whirlpool, if we find ourselves barely hanging on to our faith, let us consider a return to the basics. Let us remember that Jesus said he is the way.[16]

Instructions for Personal Reflection

Each of us comes into this retreat at a different point on the spiritual journey. As we assess where we are, we strive to recommit ourselves to the Art of Spiritual Life. Accordingly, at the end of each conference, we will provide a short reflection to be read, alone and in silence. Based on the discussion in the conference and this reflection, consider some questions that might help each of us assess our individual situation.

Reflection

St. Augustine of Hippo is one of the great Doctors of the Church. However, he spent his youth searching, seeking fulfillment in intellectual learning and carnal desires—none of which filled his inner longing. His is considered one of the great conversion stories, and his *Confessions* is a spiritual classic. He says in the opening chapter:

> You are great, Lord, and highly to be praised: Great is your power and your wisdom is immeasurable. Man, a little piece of your creation, desires to praise you, a human being 'bearing his mortality with him', carrying with him the witness of his sin and the witness that you 'resist the proud'. Nevertheless, to praise you is the desire of man, a little piece of your creation. You stir man to take pleasure in praising you, because you have

16   Cf. John 14:6. "Jesus said to him, 'I am the way and the truth and the life. No one comes to the Father except through me."

made us for yourself, and our heart is restless until it rests in you.[17]

Consider two ideas that St. Augustine has raised. First, humanity desires to praise God. Second, in a very famous passage, he wrote, "our heart is restless," which is a reality of the human experience, and this restlessness can only be satisfied by God.

Contrast this to what St. Theophan the Recluse wrote to a young woman under his spiritual guidance:

> When the spiritual reigns supreme in someone, then although this is his exclusive character and attitude, he does not err. This is because, in the first place, spirituality is the norm of the human life, and so as a result, being spiritual, he is a real person. Secondly, no matter how spiritual someone is, he cannot help but give the intellectual and carnal their rightful place; he maintains just a little of them, in subordination to the spirit. Let intellectuality not be too broad within him (in scientific knowledge, arts, and other subjects), and let carnality be firmly restrained—then he is a real, whole person. But the man of intellect (the expert, the connoisseur, the shrewd man)—and even more so the carnal man—is not a real person, no matter how appealing he seems outwardly. He is foolish. Hence the simple man who fears God is superior to the man who is diverse and elegant, but who does not have among his goals and yearnings the pleasing of God. You may judge in the same way about works of literature and art. Works in which everything is carnal are completely bad; those in which intellectuality is supreme also do not answer their purpose, although

---

17 St. Augustine of Hippo, *Confessions*, trans. Henry Chadwick (New York, NY: Oxford University Press, 2008), 3. Author's note: There are many translations of the *Confessions*. This is by far the best to read.

they are higher than the carnal. This judgment concerns those works that have no spiritual elements; those that are directly hostile toward all that is spiritual, that is, toward God and all divine things, are direct suggestions of the enemy and should not be tolerated.

From this you see that according to the natural purpose, man must live in the spirit, subordinate everything to the spirit, be penetrated by the spirit in all that is of the soul, and even more so in all that is physical—and beyond these, in the outward things, too, that is, family and social life. This is the norm![18]

Note St. Theophan's observation: "Spirituality is the norm of human life." Not the intellectual or the carnal, the pursuit of which leads to the restlessness that St. Augustine described. Only the spiritual God-centered life, will satisfy.

Reflection Questions

Spend some time with the two opening questions of this retreat:

1. What do I truly desire in life? Consider the evidence: What do I prioritize? Where do I spend my time? What friends do I associate with? What is my North Star that drives me day-in and day-out?

2. Is my faith important to me? Consider the evidence: Where does my faith fit in with my priorities? How much time do I dedicate to it? Do I think daily about my divinely created purpose? Have I drifted from the path? Is there a fire in my heart for Jesus Christ? Or, has my heart grown cold? Am I simply going through the motions?

18 St. Theophan the Recluse, *The Spiritual Life: And How to be Attuned to It*, trans. Alexandra Dockham (Safford, AZ: The Holy Monastery of St. Paisius, 2017), 59-60.

Try GOD.

If you don't like him, Satan will always take you back.

Preparing the Way

"The kingdom of God is at hand. Repent, and believe in the gospel."
(Mark 1:15)

"Repentance is the mother of life." [19]
(St. Isaac the Syrian)

Introduction

To recalibrate on the spiritual journey, we must turn to Jesus and consider the basics. His first commandment was "Repent!" This will be our starting point as well. This concept was so important to the Gospel that the preparation for the coming of the Messiah as foretold by John the Baptist focused on the same theme. Consider this in the context of the two ways: With God or without God. Repentance involves returning to God,[20] choosing to walk with him. With this in mind, we begin our second conference.

Opening Gospel Reading: The Preaching of John

Luke 3:1-6

A reading from the Holy Gospel according to St. Luke.

In the fifteenth year of the reign of Tiberius Caesar, when Pontius Pilate was governor of Judea, and Herod was tetrarch of Galilee, and his brother Philip tetrarch of

---

19 *The Ascetical Homilies of Saint Isaac the Syrian*, rev. 2nd ed. (Boston: Holy Transfiguration Monastery, 2011), 447. Homily 64.
20 See Joel 2:12. "Return to me with your whole heart, with fasting, weeping, and mourning."

the region of Ituraea and Trachonitis, and Lysanias was tetrarch of Abilene, during the high priesthood of Annas and Caiaphas, the word of God came to John the son of Zechariah in the desert. He went throughout the whole region of the Jordan, proclaiming a baptism of repentance for the forgiveness of sins, as it is written in the book of the words of the prophet Isaiah:

"A voice of one crying out in the desert: 'Prepare the way of the Lord, make straight his paths. Every valley shall be filled and every mountain and hill shall be made low. The winding roads shall be made straight, and the rough ways made smooth, and all flesh shall see the salvation of God."

The Gospel of the Lord.

Repentance

Whether we have lost the baptismal zeal in our hearts or find ourselves lost on the intermediate stage toward our destiny, repentance generally is the reset we need to recalibrate. We all have valleys to fill, mountains and hills to be made low, roads to be straightened, and rough ways that need to be made smooth again. As John the Baptist taught, preparation is necessary for salvation. St. John Climacus wrote, "Repentance is the renewal of baptism and is a contract with God for a fresh start in life."[21] Concerning the latter, we need repentance and tears for our inner life to bear fruit.[22] Thus, repentance is our starting point and a prerequisite to progress in the spiritual life. We desire to return to the Lord, to live a life pleasing to him.

Repentance stands at the forefront of cultivating a spirit of humility

---

21 St. John Climacus, *The Ladder of Divine Ascent*, trans. Colm Luibheid and Norman Russell (New York, NY: Paulist Press, 1982), 121. Step 5: On Penitence.
22 See *The Ascetical Homilies of St. Isaac the Syrian*, 201. Homily 14.

and becoming increasingly aware of the presence of God in our lives. Combined with prayer, fasting, and almsgiving, it allows us to prevail in the inevitable spiritual struggles. True repentance is the proven, all-powerful medicine offered by the Divine Physician that can transform vessels of the Devil into vessels of the Holy Spirit.[23] St. Augustine of Hippo captured this sentiment well: "You are my physician, I your patient. You are merciful; I stand in need of mercy."[24]

For the Eastern Christian, repentance is more than simply going to Confession, albeit participating in Sacramental Confession is pivotal. Rather, it is a state of mind associated with our constant striving for incremental transformation, to be increasingly Christ-like, often referred to as deification or *theosis*.[25] Accordingly, the spiritual practice of repentance could be illustrated by these four steps:

Examination > Confession > Communion >
Sober Vigilance (Watchfulness)

1. Examination

If we believe Jesus is the way to the Father, then we must periodically consider how our lives align with his. How well are we performing the will of the Father? At least daily, we should examine our lives and consider how we have followed the Divine Commandments. Abba Isaiah of Scetis wrote, "Always examine where you falter, and try to correct

---

23 Cf. St. Ignatius Brianchaninov, *The Field: Cultivating Salvation*, trans. Nicholas Kotar (Jordanville, NY: Holy Trinity Monastery Publications, 2016), 217-8.

24 St. Augustine of Hippo, *Confessions*, in *The Liturgy of the Hours*, vol. 3 (New York, NY: Catholic Book Publishing Co., 1975), 274.

25 See *The Didache Bible: With Commentaries Based on the Catechism of the Catholic Church*, 1st ed. (San Francisco, CA: Ignatius Press, 2015), 651. Commentary on Psalm 51: "Conversion is not the work or need of a moment but a continuous process by which the person not only becomes more faithful to moral law but also replicates the sentiments and deeds of Christ." See also *Catechism of the Catholic Church*, 2nd ed. (Libreria Editrice Vaticana, 1997), no. 1428. "This endeavor of conversion is not just a human work. It is the movement of a 'contrite heart,' drawn and moved by grace to respond to the merciful love of God who loved us first." And no. 1850: "Sin is thus 'love of oneself even to contempt of God.' In this proud self-exultation, sin is diametrically opposed to the obedience of Jesus, which achieves our salvation."

yourselves, asking God with pain of heart, tears, and much toil, to forgive you and keep you henceforth from falling again in the same way."[26]

A monk, through obedience, places all his acts, thoughts, and desires under the scrutiny of an Elder. Each evening, the monk comes to the Elder to discuss the conditions of his inner life and what happened during the day. Difficulties, temptations, and upheavals are the norm of anyone striving for holiness. Without such daily confession of thoughts, we can never learn to be victorious in the spiritual arena.[27]

While we may not have spiritual elders, daily confession before Jesus with compunction and sincerity of heart is a minimum. Through such regular examination and scrutiny, we begin to see how our lives are flawed and recognize our many subtle failings: the momentary flare of anger when another driver cuts us off in traffic and the habitual expletive that follows; impatience with co-workers when they take longer to understand an instruction than we believe necessary; judging a person's behavior in church or performance at work; disparaging a particular group of individuals, such as undocumented workers or the unvaccinated; criticizing others who do not live up to our self-perceived standards; failing to apply ourselves to a task at hand; entertaining impure thoughts; revisiting the photo album and fondly recalling previous sinful behaviors. These instances are small weeds that sprout up within our hearts, which, if left unchecked through complacency, can ultimately choke our hearts, causing them to turn away from God and leading to death. Nothing would delight the Devil more. And some of the Holy Fathers warn us that the accumulation of many small

---

26   Abba Isaiah of Scetis, *Ascetic Discourses*, trans. John Chryssavgis and Pachomios Penkett (Kalamazoo, MI: Cistercian Publications, 2002), 39-40.

27   Cf. Archimandrite Cherubim Karambelas, *Contemporary Ascetics of Mount Athos*, vol. 1, trans. from the Greek (Platina, CA: St. Herman of Alaska Brotherhood, 2000), 72.

sins is often more dangerous than larger ones because they slowly erode the foundation, dulling one's consciousness of such sins, and increasing habitual sinfulness. Consider the warning of Archimandrite Seraphim Aleksiev:

> The small sins are often more dangerous than the greatest crimes, because the latter weigh heavily on the conscience and insist on being atoned for, confessed, settled, erased, while the small sins do not weigh too much on the soul, but they have the perilous property of making it insensitive to the grace of God and indifferent to salvation. Fewer people have perished from ferocious beasts than have from small microbes, invisible to the naked eye. By being considered insignificant, the small sins are usually passed by without any attention. They are easily forgotten, but they create in man the most terrible habit—the habit of sinning, of dulling his moral consciousness. Thus, the wretched sinner comes to deceive himself that he is not sinful ….[28]

We often find certain habits that are hard to break, wounds hard to heal, and vivid, fond recollection of past memories. As Archimandrite Zacharias of Essex said, "It is like when we weed the fields: we take out the weeds and they come up again, but it is better to do it regularly than to leave the weeds to drown the wheat."[29] Thus, we regularly examine our lives to create greater awareness of our faults, failings, and habits to strive for incremental improvement. We should do this type

---

28 Archimandrite Seraphim Aleksiev, *The Forgotten Medicine: The Mystery of Repentance*, transl. Ralitsa Doynova (Wildwood, CA: St. Xenia Skete, 2006), 32.

29 Archimandrite Zacharias Zacharou, *The Hidden Man of the Heart (1 Peter 3:4): The Cultivation of the Heart in Orthodox Christian Anthropology*, ed. Christopher Veniamin (Waymart, PA: Mount Thabor Publishing, 2008), 59.

of examination daily; however, in the writings of the Holy Fathers, one will even see recommendations for multiple times per day.[30]

It is worth noting that the Holy Fathers advised their disciples to confess not just sinful actions but even when they simply thought about going astray. Our sins generally originate with images that the demons implant in our minds and upon which we act.[31] When a thought enters our consciousness, do we dismiss it, or do we begin to entertain the thought? St. Theophan the Recluse wrote, "Our guilt begins from the point when we favorably incline ourselves toward a passion that has been observed; that is, we do not rush to acknowledge the enemy and do not arm ourselves against it."[32] Thus, in our regular examination, we want to address those first movements in our hearts that could cause us to fall away from the narrow way.

When we examine our actions, what do we observe? What are the root causes of our sins? Is the music we listen to God-pleasing or do the lyrics spew garbage? Are the TV shows we watch God-pleasing, or do they glamorize sin? Do our friends increase our zeal for God, or keep us bound to earth or sinful behaviors? Is what we read God-pleasing; does it encourage growth in the spiritual life, or is it steeped in the ways of the world? These are just a few examples—we likely do not even realize the full extent of our vulnerabilities.

---

30 See as an example St. Dorotheos of Gaza, *Discourses and Sayings*, trans. Eric P. Wheeler (Kalamazoo, MI: Cistercian Publications, 1977), 175. Discourse XI: On Cutting Off Passionate Desires. "We really need to scrutinize our conduct every six hours and see in what way we have sinned since we sin so much and are so forgetful."

31 It is important to understand, the demons do act for us or cause us to act. They merely provide the temptation, the idea, and/or encouragement; however, we remain culpable for falling for this duplicity.

32 St. Theophan the Recluse, *The Spiritual Life*, 225.

2. Confession

Regular examination and reflection on our sinful behaviors prepare us for a formal confession before a priest to seek absolution—a rite some question as necessary. Consider St. Gregory Palamas's homily on the cleansing of the ten lepers.[33] First, St. Gregory reminds us that Jesus "graciously willed to bow the heavens and come down from on high to our lowest state to cleanse us from our sins."[34] He tells us that the hidden meaning of leprosy is sin,[35] and Jesus's instruction to the lepers who sought pity was a single commandment: "Go show yourselves to the priests."[36] Thus, St. Gregory observed:

> The obligation to demonstrate cleansing from it to the priests obviously makes it clear that none of those who have sinned against God, even if they give up sin and make amends for it through works of repentance, can receive forgiveness on their own or take their place with the blameless, unless they go to him who has authority from God to remit sins, show him, through confession, their soul eaten away by the leprosy of sin, and receive full assurance of forgiveness from him.[37]

In other words, we alone cannot declare ourselves "clean" from sin. We need the confirmation of another,[38] namely one who has been given the authority to do so by God.

---

33 See Luke 17:12-19.
34 *Saint Gregory Palamas: The Homilies*, 504. Homily Sixty-One, no. 2.
35 Ibid., 505. No. 4.
36 Luke 17:14.
37 *Saint Gregory Palamas: The Homilies*, 505. Homily Sixty-One, no. 5.
38 Ibid., See no. 4. "For the (Levitical) law laid down that a leper who had been cleansed could not bear witness to the fact himself, but had to approach the priests, show them every part of his body, and receive confirmation from them that he should be considered clean."

Sacramental Confession is essential to our interior healing, and we, too, need to obey the commandment of Jesus: "Go show yourselves to the priest."

Being thorough in Confession is important; we must own up to all our faults and failings. As St. John Climacus tells us, "In fact nothing gives demons and evil thoughts such power over us as to nourish them and hide them in our hearts unconfessed."[39] Thus, we want to empty our hearts of all our sins. Elder Cleopa of Sihastria warns us:

> The priest absolves only what he hears; the other sins remain bound to the person, for he was not sincere and will find no recourse to be relieved of this burden than through sincere confession. So, we see here another prerequisite for someone to make a thorough confession is that it must be sincere and pure.[40]

When pulling weeds from a garden, we want to remove the whole weed to prevent it from reemerging. We must not consciously hide anything, water down our failings, or hold back. Further, we cannot blame others for our sins, nor should we confess the sins of others. The unconfessed sin cannot be forgiven because the priest has not heard it and, accordingly, cannot provide absolution. Thus, we allow a poisonous weed to remain where it will proliferate. As one Athonite confessor lovingly told penitents:

> Come, my child, come. Tell me what you have done. See the icon of Christ? Don't hide anything. The Lord knows everything,

---

39 Climacus, *The Ladder*, 211. Step 23: On Pride.
40 Ioanichie Balan, *Elder Cleopa of Sihastria in the Tradition of St. Paisius Velichkovsky*, trans. Mother Cassina (Lake George, CO: New Varatec Publishing, 2001), 159.

sees everything. And I am a man of the same
passions as you. So take courage.[41]

Regular, frequent Sacramental Confession is of great
benefit to those who desire to maintain a deeper relationship
with Christ. It keeps our focus on the path to holiness. Elder
Cleopa of Sihastria said:

> Anyone who takes on the practice of confessing
> often does not allow the rust of sin to settle on
> his mind and heart. Someone who weeds his
> field often can readily tell when sin entangles
> him, and he immediately pulls it out of his
> soul through confession, This person will not
> be taken by death unprepared.[42]

3. Holy Communion

Several Holy Fathers describe the reception of Holy
Communion as a vital part of repentance. They emphasize
that Communion strengthens one's resolve to sin no more and
avoid the occasions of sin. As St. Nikodimos the Hagiorite
wrote:

> While confession and fulfilling one's ascetical
> rule is able to forgive sins, divine Communion
> is also necessary. One first removes the worms
> from a fetid wound, then cuts away the rotten
> skin and finally applies ointment to it so that
> it may heal—for if it is left untreated, it reverts
> to its former condition—and the same is true

41 Cf. Archimandrite Cherubim Karambelas, *Contemporary Ascetics of Mount Athos*, vol. 2,
    trans. from the Greek (Platina, CA: St. Herman of Alaska Brotherhood, 2000), 567, 575-576.
    The author speaks of Elder Codratus of Karakallou (1859-1940). Karakallou is one of the
    monasteries on Mount Athos. Note, too, that in the Eastern Christian tradition, the penitent
    generally faces an icon of Christ while confessing his sins during Sacramental Confession.
42 Balan, *Elder Cleopa of Sihastria*, 161.

in the case of sin. Confession removes the worms, fulfilling one's rule cuts away the dead skin, and divine Communion heals it as an ointment. For if divine Communion is not also applied, the poor sinner reverts to his former condition, 'and the last state of that man becomes worse than the first.'[43]

This imagery is worth noting. Confession addresses the wound itself, removing the rot and worms, and Eucharist is the healing ointment. In other words, drawing back to Christ provides complete healing and restoration. Both Confession and Communion are required. St. Nikodemos adds:

After one receives Communion, he thinks about the dread and heavenly Mysteries of which he partook, and so he takes heed to himself so as not to dishonor that grace. He fears his thoughts, shrinks away from them, and protects himself from them. He begins a more correct and virtuous life, and, as much as is possible, abstains from every evil. When he begins to think about the fact that he will be receiving Communion again in just a few days, he doubles his efforts to watch over himself. He adds zeal to zeal, self-control to self-control, vigilance to vigilance, labors upon labors, and he struggles as much as possible. This is because he is pressed on two sides: on one side, because just a short while ago he received Communion, and on the other, because he will receive again in just a short while.[44]

---

43   St. Nikodimos the Hagiorite, *Concerning Frequent Communion of the Immaculate Mysteries of Christ*, trans. George Dokos (Thessaloniki, Greece: Uncut Mountain Press, 2006), 121. Reference to Matt. 12:45.
44   Ibid., 122.

St. Nikodimos envisaged Eucharist as reinforcing repentance, both rekindling the interior life with the presence of Christ and reinforcing the promise to avoid the occasions of sin, especially when one soon wants to receive Communion again. Elder Ambrose of Optina advised, "After receiving Communion, you must ask the Lord to grant you to preserve it worthily, and ask the Lord to grant you help not to turn back, that is, to your former sins."[45] Thus, certain Holy Fathers consider Holy Communion as a necessary step in the process of repentance.

4. Sober Vigilance / Watchfulness

Many Holy Fathers stress the importance of guarding one's heart,[46] which is often referred to as watchfulness or vigilance (nepsis). This brings the process of repentance full circle because one means of guarding the heart is frequent examination of where breaches occur. This should also lead to avoiding the occasions of sin—not placing ourselves in positions of temptation and vulnerability. For example, an alcoholic generally does not socialize at a bar where the risk of giving into temptation is significantly increased. St. Mark the Ascetic wrote, "Sin is a blazing fire. The less fuel you give it, the faster it dies down; the more you feed it, the more it burns."[47]

While confession restores our baptismal state of grace and we are forgiven, our souls remain weakened by past sinful habits. "Just as a worm eats away at wood and destroys it, evil

---

45 Fr. Sergius Chetverikov, *Elder Ambrose of Optina*, "The Optina Elders Series," vol. 4, trans. from the Russian (Platina, CA: St. Herman of Alaska Brotherhood, 2009), 232.

46 See John Chryssavgis, "Introduction," *Abba Isaiah of Scetis: Ascetic Discourses* (Kalamazoo, MI: Cistercian Publications, 2002), 37.

47 St. Mark the Ascetic, "On the Spiritual Law: Two Hundred Texts," *The Philokalia: The Complete Text*, vol. 1, comp. St. Nikodimos of the Holy Mountain and St. Makarios of Corinth, trans. G.E.H. Palmer, P. Sherrard, and K. Ware (London: Faber & Faber, 1979), 118.

in the heart darkens the soul."[48] We cannot neglect our souls even for a day. The temptations and passions are relentless and sometimes we find ourselves, as St. Theophan the Recluse described it, led along like a young donkey on a cord behind its owner.[49] Through repentance, we strive to loosen the passions' grip on us, the bad habits that have become engrained, choosing instead the path to holiness and restoring our natural state, which is spiritual. Accordingly, we must be ever-vigilant because it is easy to fall back into sinful ways. There is a reason the Holy Fathers call it spiritual *warfare*, a constant struggle for our salvation. St. John Climacus wrote:

> Do not be surprised if you fall every day and do not surrender. Stand your ground bravely. And you may be sure that your guardian angel will respect your endurance. A fresh, warm wound is easier to heal than those that are old, neglected, and festering, and that need extensive treatment, surgery, bandaging, and cauterization. Long neglect can render many of them incurable. However, all things are possible with God.[50]

When we grow weary from such vigilance and struggle, which requires significant effort, we become complacent and are vulnerable.

Importance of a Father-Confessor

We cannot rely on ourselves because of our fallen human nature, especially with judgments and decisions relative to the spiritual

---

48   Abba Isaiah of Scetis, *Ascetic Discourses*, 124. Discourse 16.
49   Cf. St. Theophan the Recluse, *The Spiritual Life*, 215.
50   Climacus, *The Ladder*, 130. Step 5: On Penitence. Reference to Matt. 19:26.

life. As with the case of the ten lepers, we cannot simply declare ourselves clean. In an ideal world, we would find an unerring spiritual father. However, in reality, such guides are few and far between. So, at a minimum, we should seek a good father-confessor and find strength in the sacramental life of the Church. It is good to have one priest to whom we can consistently go, who knows us and provides appropriate spiritual counsels. Further, as a penitent going to the same priest, we hold ourselves to greater accountability in avoiding sinful behavior. Some may go to

an unknown priest when their sin is great, and they feel embarrassed to disclose it. This is all the more reason to go to a single father-confessor. In fact, in some Orthodox jurisdictions, deliberately confessing to a different priest in such a situation is considered sinful! It is not unlike hiding a sin.[51]

Our downfall is self-will and a self-directed spiritual life because, as St. Macarius the Great said, we all retain at least a grain of pride. We have blind spots and personal filters that impair our ability to make progress in the interior life. Accordingly, we need an outside perspective provided by a good father-confessor who can more readily see us as we truly are.

---

51 As clarification, many Spiritual Fathers would say that in the case of serious sin, it should be confessed immediately. If one's father-confessor is not available, they suggest confessing to a priest to avoid remaining in a state of sin, but then disclosing it to one's father-confessor as well.

Despair

One of the most effective weapons used by the Devil is despair, especially when a person gives into the belief that they are unforgiveable. Elder Leonid of Optina said, "Despondency torments everyone, it destroys the solitary fruits of sobriety in even the greatest men."[52] Simply put, no sin is beyond the mercy of God. Consider Jesus's forgiveness of the woman caught in the act of adultery, or St. Paul's conversion after having approved the stoning of St. Stephen. There are many stories of conversion, wherein great sinners have become saints. Consider St. Augustine of Hippo, Dorothy Day, or Jacques Fesch, a convicted murderer who had a profound conversion in prison before his execution. No one is beyond the mercy of God. To think otherwise is a denial of God and, in essence, blasphemy—the unpardonable sin against the Holy Spirit[53]—because it is the sinner himself who prevents God from forgiving him. The Devil would like people to believe they are beyond the grace of God; however, the depth and fullness of God's mercy cannot be judged with human understanding, which is flawed and limited.

Conclusion

A spirit of repentance is foundational for growth in the spiritual life. We are all called to holiness; however, our human nature is weak. Our immersive culture encourages and sometimes tacitly endorses behavior contrary to the teachings of Jesus. It is easy to go along with the crowd, knowingly or unconsciously choosing the way without God. "Repentance signifies a firm resolution not to return to sin."[54] As such, it is not simply an event-driven activity, such as Sacramental

---

52 Fr. Clement Sederholm, *Elder Leonid of Optina*, "The Optina Elders Series," vol. 1, trans. from Russian (Platina, CA: St. Herman of Alaska Brotherhood, 2002), 188. Sobriety in this context is watchfulness or vigilance against the potential encroachments of sin.

53 Cf. Matt. 12:31.

54 *The Evergetinos: The Complete Text,* vol. 1, trans. Archbishop Chrysostomos and Hieromonk Patapios (Etna, CA: Center for Traditionalist Orthodox Studies, 2008), vol. 1, 6. Hypothesis I: No one should despair ever, even if he has committed many sins, but should have hope that, through repentance, he shall be saved.

Confession. Instead, it is our means of following Jesus more closely, avoiding the occasions and temptations of sin, ascending spiritually, and cultivating meekness, humility, and purity of heart.[55] It is a deliberate effort to free ourselves from the yoke of the passions, becoming the people we were created to be, and renouncing that which is contrary to the teachings of the Gospel.

No one said the spiritual journey would be easy. Jesus told us that those who wish to follow him must deny themselves, taking up their crosses daily and following him.[56] It is not a life of ease. Rather, we strive with great pain and suffering to show God that we desire him above all else and renounce any bonds that prevent a deeper relationship with him.

Will we fall? Most likely, yes, because our human nature is weak. The moment we choose to follow Christ, we enter into an arena of intense spiritual struggle in which the demons deploy a variety of clever tactics to pull us away from the path to salvation. These include (1) vivid remembrance of passions and how pleasant they seemed,[57] a veritable photo album of enticement, (2) despair (*God could not possibly want a sinner such as me.*),[58] (3) complacency (*You've done well; it is okay to take a break; treat yourself*), and (4) delusion (*You are better than most, so do not worry*). Repentance involves continuously groaning from the depths of our hearts, mourning our past sins and striving to try anew. In addition, we must always remember that the compassion, mercy, and love of God are greater than any sin we have committed or type of lifestyle we have led. The Prodigal Son was welcomed back with love and mercy.[59] Once we repent and confess, the slate is wiped clean, period. God looks for even the smallest movement in the heart to draw a person back to him, embracing us

---

55   Cf. Matt. 5:8. "Blessed are the clean (pure) of heart, for they will see God."
56   See Luke 9:23.
57   See *The Evergetinos*, vol. 1, 2.
58   Ibid.
59   See Luke 15:11-32. Parable of the Prodigal Son.

like the Forgiving Father did the Prodigal.[60] "Let us abandon the evil one and his herds. Let us keep away from the pigs and the husks they eat, that is to say, the disgusting passions and their devotees."[61] The Father awaits us!

Reflection

From Elder Palladios in *The Evergetinos*:

> There once lived in the city, it was said, a young man who committed many and frightful sins. However, this young man was piercingly censured by his conscience, on account of his manifold sins, and with the help of God came to repentance. Under the power of repentance, he went to a cemetery where he established himself in one of the tombs[62] and lamented for his former life, falling down with his face to the earth and continually groaning from the depth of his heart.
>
> When he had passed a week in this state of unrelenting and persistent repentance, the demons, who had before brought his life to destruction, gathered around one night making noise and shouting: 'Who is this impious man, who used to pass his time in lustful things and immorality, yet now wants us to think that he is sober and a doer of good deeds? And he wants to be a Christian and become virtuous, now that he can no longer have fun and fulfill his pleasures? What

---

60 See Luke 15:20. "While he was still a long way off, his father caught sight of him, and was filled with compassion. He ran to his son, embraced him and kissed him."
61 *St. Gregory Palamas: The Homilies*, 23. Homily Three.
62 Recall that St. Antony of Egypt also originally took up a dwelling in a tomb where he was severely tested and tormented by the demons. See St. Athanasius of Alexandria, "The Life of Antony of Egypt," in *The Wisdom of the Desert Fathers and Mothers*, trans. Henry I. Carrigan, Jr. (Brewster, MA: Paraclete Press), 10-13. Nos. 9-11.

good can he expect in his life, since he is filled with our evils?'

'Hey you! Will you not get up from there at all? Will you not come with us to your customary places of sin and depravity? Fallen women and wine await you— will you not come to indulge your desires? After all the sins you have committed up to this day, all hope for salvation is lost to you, and therefore, O struggler, you will only march on full speed to your damnation if you continue killing yourself in this way. Why are you so intent and in such a hurry to be damned? Whatever transgression that there is, you committed it; together with us, you fell to every sin. Yet now you dare to flee our company? Do you not agree? Will not go along with our offers?'

Meanwhile, however, the young man persisted in the sorrow of repentance and, appearing not to hear the exhortations of the demons, did not answer them at all. So the demons, seeing that they had accomplished nothing with their words, fell upon him, beat him cruelly, and when they had thoroughly wounded him, left him half-dead. But still the youth remained immovable in his place, groaning but steadfast in his inexorable repentance.

During this time, the young man's relatives sought him out, finally, finding him. Having learned the reason for his appearance—that is, of the brazen attack of the demons—they tried to take him with them to their home. He, however, refused to abandon the place of his repentance.

The following night, the demons again attacked him and tormented him even more greatly. His relatives visited him a second time, though without persuading him to leave his place of punishment and follow them. To their proposals on the matter, he answered patiently and with resignation: 'Do not pressure me. I prefer to die than to return to my former prodigal life.'

The third night he almost died from the cruel torments of the demons, who attacked him with greater severity than all of the other times.

After that, the demons, having accomplished nothing with their threats and torments—for the young man would not change his mind at any scare tactic—departed him and left him alone.

Fleeing from him, they cried madly: 'He conquered us! He conquered us! He conquered us!'

From that time on, nothing bad happened to the youth; rather, with a clean conscience he came to realize every virtue. Until the end of his life, he remained in the tomb, which he made his hermitage, coming to be honored by God with the gifts of miraculous deeds.[63]

Reflection Questions

1. We discussed Repentance as a way of life having four specific practices: (1) Examination, (2) Sacramental Confession, (3)

---

63   See *The Evergetinos,* vol. 1, 1-2.

Holy Communion, and (4) Vigilance. Which of these practices have I cultivated? Which do I need to cultivate further? Why?

2. Do I find myself repeatedly falling into the same sins? What I can I do to break the vicious cycle?

3. What changes do I need to make to live a more God-pleasing life?

Further Reading

We highly recommend the following short book, which is a spiritual gem.

Aleksiev, Archimandrite Seraphim. *The Forgotten Medicine: The Mystery of Repentance*. Translated by Ralitsa Doynova. Wildwood, CA: St. Xenia Skete, 2006.

Icon of the Parable of the Prodigal Son

Do we recognize our need for repentance and forgiveness? Or, do we desire to remain in the pigpen or find ourselves returning to the pigpen?

Remaining on the Narrow Way

"What comes out of a person, that is what defiles."
(Mark 7:20)

"A person may consent to evil for years, and nothing happens. Unknown to him, his freedom diminishes, his body weakens, and his will becomes atrophied." [64]
(Servant of God Jacques Fesch)

"All the evil begins when a person gives into his imagination and allows sinful thoughts to prevail."
(Elder Ephraim of Arizona)

Opening Thought

Whoever chooses to follow Christ will immediately step into an arena of immense and seemingly-overwhelming unseen warfare where the demons will deploy any tactic to derail the person's relationship with God. In the reflection from the last conference, we read how unrelenting the assaults of these demons can be. It reminds us that we must be ever vigilant, standing our ground, and not consenting to sin.

Opening Gospel Reading: That Which Defiles

Mark 7:14-23

A reading from the Holy Gospel according to St. Mark.

---

64 Augustin-Michel Lemonnier, *Light Over the Scaffold: Prison Letters of Jacques Fesch* and *Cell 18: Unedited Letters of Jacques Fesch*, trans. Sr. Mary Thomas Noble, OP (Staten Island, NY: Society of St, Paul, 1996), 80.

Jesus summoned the crowd again and said to them, 'Hear me, all of you, and understand. Nothing that enters one from outside can defile that person; but the things that come out from within are what defile.'

When he got home away from the crowd his disciples questioned him about the parable. He said to them, 'Are even you likewise without understanding? Do you not realize that everything that goes into a person from outside cannot defile, since it enters not the heart but the stomach and passes out into the latrine?' (Thus he declared all foods clean.) 'But what comes out of a person, that is what defiles. From within people, from their hearts, come evil thoughts, unchastity, theft, murder, adultery, greed, malice, deceit, licentiousness, envy, blasphemy, arrogance, folly. All these evils come from within and they defile.'

The Gospel of the Lord

Detecting Breaches

In the process of repentance, we discussed the importance of vigilance in avoiding the occasions of sin and repeating sinful actions resulting from ingrained behaviors. We must remain on guard at all times, not becoming drowsy or negligent. In reality, we rarely experience an all-out assault from the demons—like the Devil tempting Jesus saying, "Prostrate yourself and worship me."[65] Such an attack is more easily recognizable, and the demons are far stealthier in their attempts to breach our defenses. Rather, they try to shift our focus on autonomy and self-interest, which are our greatest weaknesses, where what I want triumphs over what God wants. We

---

65   Matt. 4:9.

have noted that our sins generally originate with images and thoughts implanted in our minds. Let us consider this further.

Being made in the image of God, humanity was endowed with reason, which includes rational thought. Elder Thaddeus of Vitovnica taught:

> Our life depends on the kind of thoughts we nurture.
> If our thoughts are peaceful, calm, meek, and kind,
> then that is what our life will be like. If our attention
> is turned to the circumstances in which we live, we
> are drawn into a whirlpool of thoughts and can have
> neither peace nor tranquility.[66]

An objective in the spiritual life is to seek peace and harmony with God, ourselves, and our neighbors. St. Seraphim of Sarov is known for saying, "Learn to be peaceful and thousands around you will be saved."[67] And for this reason, the demons desire to cast us into a turbulent whirlpool of concerns, worries, and other negative thoughts. Elder Thaddeus warned that the breeding of negative thoughts is a great evil.[68] However, let us consider how our thoughts can be exploited.

We need sobriety and vigilance to avoid occasions for sin. Every thought that seeks entrance into our hearts should be scrutinized to avoid a breach. Even a minor crack in our defenses can grow, and if left unchecked, result in catastrophic failure. While we may be tempted to think this could never happen to us (*I would never let something get that far*), let us consider how a negative thought can escalate to our downfall.

---

66 *Our Thoughts Determine Our Lives: The Life and Teachings of Elder Thaddeus of Vitovnica*, comp. St Herman of Alaska Brotherhood, trans. Ana Smiljanic (Platina, CA: St. Herman of Alaska Brotherhood, 2017), 63.

67 Valentine Zander, *St. Seraphim of Sarov*, trans. Sr. Gabriel Anne SSC (Crestwood, NY: St. Vladimir's Seminary Press, 1975), x.

68 *Our Thoughts Determine Our Lives*, 63.

The Narrow Gate

Hieromonk Dorofey of Konevitsa, a Russian monk, explained it as such.[69] First, an idea or image appears in our mind or heart, a provocation, perhaps a suggestion to do something. We cannot avoid having thoughts passing through our minds, even undesirable ones. Only those ascetics who have achieved great spiritual heights can avoid such thoughts and, then, only for a time. St. Mark the Ascetic explained, "A provocation does not involve us in guilt so long as it is not accompanied by images. Some people flee these thoughts like a brand plucked out of the fire; but others dally with them, and so get burned."[70]

As thoughts, provocations can be sinless—we have not yet engaged them. However, the next stage is a connection whereby we feel an attraction to the thought, not readily dismissing it; rather, we welcome it and allow it to remain. When we revisit the thought, we are starting to engage a sinful suggestion. We dally and get burned. This can then advance to the next stage, fusion, in which we begin a mental dialogue with the idea and decide to act on it. Laziness, complacency, or neglect allows such fusion to take place. If the person accepts the suggestion but soon afterward repents and confesses his sin before the Lord and invokes his assistance, God readily forgives us in his mercy. This kind of fusion can be easily forgiven.[71]

However, such fusion can continue, wherein through free will, we accept the suggestions to such a degree that we no longer resist them and decide to engage in the temptation when the opportunity arises. We may actively seek occasions, places, or situations to engage in the behavior. In this case, if the temptation is not acted upon, it is generally because the opportunity has not yet arisen. As an example, one may not be chaste for the sake of the kingdom. One may be

---

69 See Sergius Bolshakoff and M. Basil Pennington, OCSO, *In Search of True Wisdom: Visits to Eastern Spiritual Fathers* (New York, NY: Alba House, 1979), 29-32. Hieromonk Dorofey summarizes his understanding of the teachings of St. Nilus of Sora (Nil Sorsky), the five stages from thought to sin, with which many of the Russian Fathers were familiar.
70 St. Mark the Ascetic, "On the Spiritual Law," 120. Reference to Zech 3:2.
71 Ibid., 30.

chaste because the opportunity to pursue an impure relationship did not yet present itself. These are not the same, and we delude ourselves if we believe that we can remain without sin.

The next stage is imprisonment. "Our heart is irresistibly attracted to the seducing thought. We retain it within us. We carry on a mental discussion with the idea, which disturbs our whole spiritual life."[72] In a situation like a desire for revenge for a wrong, our mind can be overwhelmed by a tempest, making it impossible to return to our former peace and quiet. The sinful thought now manifests itself during our prayer, during church services, and other times, becoming increasingly obsessive. This can lead to further inclination, reviving a sinful habit, and atrophy of heart and soul. It can lead to neglect of prayer through continuous preoccupation. "Thus a drunkard continually thinks of when and how he can obtain his drink, the fornicator is obsessed with women, and the worrisome person with his money, and so on."[73] This monk's description shows how we can be easily overwhelmed through thoughts that we allow into our hearts without proper checks and balances. If such a thought, for example, readily disturbs our prayer or spiritual activities, it has reached a serious point of escalation.

We might be tempted to dismiss our thoughts—thoughts are harmless, we may think. Yet the demons will continuously try to breach our defenses through suggestions and memories of the past; they are relentless, and we are weak. We have volumes of memories in picture books stored within our minds, so there is plenty of source material from which the demons can provide appealing suggestions. Addictions or previous sinful behaviors further increase our vulnerability to attack. Coupled with a secular society that embraces individualistic behaviors and immoral life styles—*it's okay, don't worry about it*—the risk of giving into temptation is great. We consistently need to be on the defensive. St. Paisios of Mount Athos describes it well:

---

72   Ibid., 31.
73   Ibid.

Thoughts are like airplanes flying in the air. If you ignore them, there's no problem. If you pay attention to them, you create an airport inside your head and permit them to land! If you see a thought flying like a helicopter and trying to land where it shouldn't—in other words, a persistent thought—then you take the bazooka and boom! –Then confess it. This is because the goal is to rise spiritually, not simply avoid sin.[74]

The problem is allowing the thought to land, penetrating our defenses and entering our heart. We create the airport, allowing the thought to enter rather than purging it when it is still at a distance. And when one thought or demon crosses the frontier, more are sure to follow. St. Paisios advised:

There is reason to worry when a person levels out a part of his heart to make a landing strip and accepts little devils that come to him. And if this happens once in a while, then go directly to Confession, plow up the landing strip, the mind and the heart, and plant fruit-bearing trees, to turn the heart again to Paradise.[75]

Through carelessness, we can easily be swept away with the crowd on the wide road leading to destruction. Herein, we see the importance of daily examination of conscience and confession of thoughts—not becoming complacent. When we engage the thoughts, *fusion,* in the words of Hieromonk Dorofey, we should bring these thoughts to our father-confessor in Sacramental Confession. As an example, Jesus taught, "Everyone who looks at a woman with lust has already committed adultery with her in his heart."[76]

---

74 "St. Paisios the Athonite on Spiritual Warfare," *The Ascetic Experience* online (Sept. 28, 2019). https://www.asceticexperience.com.

75 St. Paisios the Athonite, "Spiritual Struggle," *Spiritual Counsels*, vol. 3, trans. Fr. Peter Chamberas, ed. Anna Famellos and Andronikos Masters (Souroti, Thessaloniki, Greece: Holy Hesychasterion Evangelist John the Theologian, 2014), 76.

76 Matt. 5:28.

Accountability for Our Sins

We tend to blame our sinful inclinations or temptations on others. We likely have heard the classic expression, "The Devil made me do it." It is a means of dismissing accountability, which is detrimental to our spiritual life. Elder Cleopa of Sihastria said it well:

> If someone wants to sin, he sins; if he does not want to sin, he doesn't. The Devil only puts the ideas in our minds, so if someone is foolish and deceived, he commits the sin. Can you say on the day of judgment, 'Lord, the Devil took me into the bar, the Devil made me sin with such and such a woman, the Devil made me steal, the Devil made me a drunkard, the Devil made me have an abortion, etc.'? If so, then the Devil will say, 'Lord, show me a witness who saw me drag this person into the bar, or into the fornication, or murder!' Then the same Devil will turn to the man and say, 'See how foolish you are? I only suggested these sins to you. But since you are a fool, you gave yourself over to them on your own. I did not drag you! But since you listened to me, now you arc mine!'[77]

Do not be deceived! We choose to sin and should not attempt to reduce our culpability. Better to seek the healing remedy of Sacramental Confession than to persist in engaging thoughts that are harmful to our soul. Allowing such inappropriate thoughts to enter our hearts, to revisit them or engage them, is not harmless. Our defenses have been breached, and the structure is weakened. As St. Paisios would say, "It is time for the bazooka!"

---

77   Balan, *Elder Cleopa of Sihastria*, 160.

The Narrow Gate

Sobriety: Preventing Breaches

Repentance is a powerful tool to increase vigilance and sobriety. It is also an admission of our need for divine assistance, turning to God, asking for his mercy and forgiveness. Another tool against problematic thoughts, as advised by many Holy Fathers, is prayer. Elder Michael the Recluse of Valaam said:

> When a thought arises, cut it off at once with the Prayer of Jesus. If you start examining it, it will stick to you and you will get interested in it. It will chain you and you will have agreement with it and will start thinking how to fulfill it. And then you will perform it in deed, and this is how sin arises.[78]

We should also carefully consider how undesirable thoughts can be increased or aggravated. What television programs do we watch? What types of books do we read? To what music do we listen? How do we spend our spare time? When and how do we relax our defenses? "A sleeping conscience needs a strong shaking to awaken,"[79] wrote St. John of Kronstadt.

Our fallen human nature is enslaved to sin, and we are not always aware to what extent until it manifests itself in pride, anger, impatience, jealousy, judgment, ingratitude, lustful thoughts, or a variety of other negative stirrings in our heart. We will also be tormented by memories of our sinful past, tempted to return just one more time, similar to reminiscing with an old friend. It is like an alcoholic who decides to have a drink to celebrate progress after a long period of sobriety. Sinful behaviors are often like such addictions, lingering just below the surface like a trap ready to ensnare us. St. Mary of Egypt was

---

78 Nun Maria Stakhovich and Sergius Bolshakoff, *Interior Silence: Elder Michael, The Last Great Mystic of Valaam* (New Valaam Monastery, AK: St. Herman of Alaska Brotherhood, 1992), 92.

79 St. John of Kronstadt, *Ten Homilies on the Beatitudes*, trans. N. Kizenko-Frugier (Albany, NY: Corner Editions/La Pierre Angulaire, 2003), 53.

painfully afflicted by memories of her immoral, sensual life for 17 years, despite having confessed her sins and withdrawn to the desert to repent. Vivid memories are imprinted in our minds like pictures in a photo album. The demons will exploit these, torturing us and attempting to knock us off the path to holiness by encouraging us again to seek such pleasures of the past (*Just one more time; you don't do it all the time, so you are better than most*). The Holy Fathers are clear about the intensity of these struggles, which, as St. Peter of Damaskos described, reach the point of shedding blood ("give blood and receive spirit"[80]). How often do we step into the spiritual arena and find ourselves defeated? Is it any wonder we have trouble hearing the voice of Jesus over the many other voices that try to drown him out? We dismiss Jesus when he describes the way of the cross and, instead, desire to let the good times roll, attempting to forego suffering altogether.

At the same time, we also cannot despair at our weaknesses or the number of times we have fallen because the demons will exploit this, too, striving to alienate us even further from God ("*God would not possibly want a sinner like you; look where you've been.*"). Abba Moses the Black gives us an excellent example of someone who, through great ascetical struggles, finally stopped listening to the voices that tormented him—lust, fornication, debauchery—that kept beckoning him like sirens to join them on the path of destruction. Like St. Mary of Egypt or the young man in the cemetery described by Elder Palladios in *The Evergetinos*, Abba Moses was mercilessly tormented. Yet, this monk eventually tamed his passions through his ascetical struggles, was ordained a priest, became a spiritual father to others, and eventually was martyred by bandits.

> This former robber turned monk provides us with a shining example of how even the foulest and most dastardly of sinners can, through repentance and

---

80   Cited by Elder Ambrose of Optina. See Chetverikov, *Elder Ambrose of Optina*, 220.

asceticism, so purify his heart as to find freedom from the passions and gain entrance into the kingdom of God.[81]

We need to cut off the root of temptations, not unnecessarily exposing ourselves to occasions for sin, increasingly denying ourselves, and replacing our previous societally-approved activities with God-pleasing activities. We have less desire for the fruit if it is not in sight or readily available.[82] We can change our friends, the materials we read, and how we spend our time, increasing our pursuit of the spiritual life. If we truly desire the life of the world to come, we will likely need to shift our priorities. St. Paisios of Mount Athos said, "If you want to enjoy spiritual fruit, you must struggle and be patient."[83]

Finally, we need to recognize that we cannot be successful in the interior struggle on our own. We need divine assistance (*synergeia*), which is gained when we surrender our will to God's will, doing what is pleasing in his sight and allowing him to act, instead of following our own whims and designs.[84] Jesus seeks the lost and desires their redemption. There is no sin that cannot be overcome by God's overwhelming love. Like the Prodigal, we simply need to make the decision to return, to leave the land of passions, and the Father will be waiting to embrace us and restore our dignity as children of God.

---

81   Trisagion Films, *Remember Me in Your Kingdom: The Life of Abba Moses the Ethiopian* (2017).

82   Cf. Climacus, *The Ladder*, 86. Step 3: On Exile. "Run from places of sin as though from a plague. When fruit is not in plain sight you have no great urge to taste it."

83   St. Paisios the Athonite, "Passions and Virtues," *Spiritual Counsels*, vol. 5, trans. Fr. Peter Chamberas, ed. Anna Famellos and Eleftheria Kaimakliotis (Souroti, Thessaloniki, Greece: Holy Hesychasterion Evangelist John the Theologian, 2016), 297.

84   See *Unseen Warfare*: Being the *Spiritual Combat* and *Path to Paradise* of Lorenzo Scupoli, ed. Nicodemus of the Holy Mountain, rev. Theophan the Recluse, trans. E. Kadloubovsky and G. E. H. Palmer (London: Faber and Faber, 1963), 144. "In spiritual warfare, by prayer you put your battle-axe in God's hand, that he might fight your enemies and overcome them."

Reflection

From St. Hesychios the Priest:

> One type of watchfulness consists in closely scrutinizing every mental image or provocation; for only by means of a mental image can Satan fabricate an evil thought and insinuate this into the intellect to lead it astray.

> A second type of watchfulness consists in freeing the heart from all thoughts, keeping it profoundly silent and still, and in praying.

> A third type consists in continually and humbly calling upon the Lord Jesus Christ for help.

> A fourth type is always to have the thought of death in one's mind.

> These types of watchfulness, my child, act like doorkeepers and bar entry to evil thoughts ... this is to fix one's gaze on heaven and to pay no attention to anything material.

> When we have to some extent cut off the causes of the passions (habits), we should devote our time to spiritual contemplation; for if we fail to do this we shall easily revert to the fleshly passions, and so achieve nothing but the complete darkening of our intellect and its reversion to material things.

> The man engaged in spiritual warfare should simultaneously possess humility, perfect attentiveness, the power of rebuttal, and prayer. He should possess humility because, as his fight is against arrogant demons, he will then have the help of Christ in his

heart, for 'the Lord hates the arrogant' (Prov. 3:34).
He should possess attentiveness in order always to
keep his heart clear of all thoughts, even of those that
appear to be good. He should possess the power of
rebuttal so that, whenever he recognizes the Devil,
he may at once repulse him angrily; for it is written:
'And I shall reply to those who vilify me; will my soul
not be subject to God?' (Ps. 119:42; 62:1). He should
possess prayer so that as soon as he has rebutted the
Devil, he may call to Christ with 'cries that cannot
be uttered' (Rom. 8:26). Then he will see the Devil
broken and routed by the venerable name of Jesus—
will see him and his dissimulation scattered like dust
or smoke before the wind.

If we have not attained prayer that is free from
thoughts, we have no weapon to fight with. By this
prayer I mean the prayer which is ever active in the
inner shrine of the soul, and which by invoking Christ
scourges and sears our secret enemy.

The glance of your intellect should be quick and keen,
able to perceive the invading demons. When you
perceive one, you should at once rebut it, crushing
it like the head of a serpent. At the same time, call
imploringly to Christ, and you will experience God's
unseen help.[85]

85 St. Hesychios the Priest, "On Watchfulness and Holiness," in *The Philokalia: The Complete Text*, vol. 1, comp. St. Nikodimos of the Holy Mountain and St. Makarios of Corinth, trans. G.E.H. Palmer, P. Sherrard, and K. Ware (London: Faber & Faber, 1979), 164-5.

Reflection Questions

1. What is my reaction to the perspective of the Holy Fathers that our sins originate from thoughts, suggestions, or ideas that the demons implant in our minds?

2. What temptations do I experience most frequently? Are these influenced by what I watch on television, places where I spend my time, friends I keep?

3. What changes do I need to make to live a more God-pleasing life?

"How narrow the gate and constricted the road that leads to life. And those who find it are few."
(Matt. 7:14)

The Narrow Gate

Why is it that only the narrow way and narrow gate lead to life? Who makes this chosen path so narrow? The world, the Devil, and the flesh—these narrow our way into the kingdom of heaven.[86] St. Ignatius Brianchaninov wrote:

> The road leading to eternal life is narrow and full of sorrows. There are few who walk it, but it is the only road for all who wish to be saved. One should never walk away from it! Let us firmly and constantly bear any temptation that the Devil hurls at us, looking with the eyes of faith at the treasures awaiting us in heaven.
>
> No matter what sorrows we are subjected to in this earthly life, they can never be compared with the benefits that are promised us in eternity, with the consolation that the Holy Spirit gives here on earth, with the freedom from the dominion of the passions, with the forgiveness of our many debts, or with any of the inevitable consequences of our patient suffering.
>
> Why were we not subject to such insults and sufferings when we served the world and its numerous cares? Why now, when we have begun to serve God, are we subjected to so many problems? Know this: for Christ's sake are these sorrows poured on us like arrows. Our enemy, the Devil, fires them at us to take vengeance on us for the eternal blessings upon which we trust, and which we try to attain. He wishes to weaken our souls with sadness, despair, and laziness; and, in this way, to deny us our desired blessedness.
>
> Christ invisibly battles on our side. This powerful and

---

86   St. John of Kronstadt, *My Life in Christ*, Part I, trans. E. E. Goulaeff, rev. Nicholas Kotar (Jordanville, NY: Holy Trinity Monastery, 2015), 125.

matchless Mediator destroys all the tricks and traps of our enemy.

He himself, our Lord and Savior, during his entire earthly life, walked along the narrow and sorrowful path, and not on any other. He was constantly persecuted, he was beaten, laughed at, and finally, he was killed by the most shameful death possible, on the cross between two thieves.

Let us follow Christ![87]

The narrow way is difficult, and it can be very lonely. Nevertheless, we can find consolation in knowing that Christ has traveled this way before us—as have the Holy Fathers who followed his way and are our spiritual guides.

---

87   Brianchaninov, *The Field*, 288-9. Consider also the following podcast: Fr. Miron Kerul-Kmec, *The Art of Spiritual Life*, Podbean, The Field 76.

Rendering an Account

"For the Son of Man will come with his angels in his Father's glory,
and then he will repay everyone according to his conduct."
(Matt. 16:27)

"When God decides to take you, he will take you, no
matter how many safety measures you take."
(Elder Ephraim of Arizona)

Opening Thought

At some point, the intermediate stage described by St. Gregory Palamas will draw to a close, and we will find ourselves before the fearsome judgment seat of Christ, required to give an account of how we spent our lives. Jesus was unambiguous: There will be a judgment. However, because no one knows the day or hour, each of us must be ready, not putting off salvation to another day.

Opening Gospel Reading: Parable of the Great Feast

Luke 14:15-24

A reading from the Holy Gospel according to St. Luke.

One of his fellow guests … said to [Jesus], "Blessed is the one who will dine in the kingdom of God."

He replied to him, "A man gave a great dinner to which he invited many. When the time for the dinner came, he dispatched his servant to say to those invited,

'Come, everything is now ready.' But one by one, they all began to excuse themselves. The first said to him, 'I have purchased a field and must go to examine it; I ask you, consider me excused.' And another said, 'I have purchased five yoke of oxen and am on my way to evaluate them; I ask you, consider me excused.' And another said, 'I have just married a woman, and therefore I cannot come.'

"The servant went and reported this to his master. Then the master of the house in a rage commanded his servant, 'Go out quickly into the streets and alleys of the town and bring in here the poor and the crippled, the blind and the lame.'

"The servant reported, 'Sir, your orders have been carried out and still there is room.' The master then ordered the servant, 'Go out to the highways and hedgerows and make people come in that my home may be filled.

'For, I tell you, none of those men who were invited will taste my dinner.'"

The Gospel of the Lord.

Convinced of Our Own Invincibility

A classic scene in the movie *Titanic* finds Leonardo DiCaprio's character, Jack Dawson, standing on the bow of the great ship shouting, "I'm the king of the world!" Many are filled with such youthful enthusiasm, believing in their innate abilities and invincibility. Yet this can lead to two delusions. The first is postponing a response to Jesus's invitation or, worse, outright dismissal of the need for salvation. No one knows the time or hour when one is called from this life. As forewarned by St. Gregory Palamas, the famine of today occurs "when someone is deprived of the necessary means of salvation and does not perceive his misfortune, having no desire to be saved."[88]

The second is believing in a self-directed life where we decide to be our own guides, thinking we know best—a disastrous approach to the spiritual journey given our flawed human nature. True pursuit of eternal blessedness with God requires a surrender of self-will to the divine will, and appropriate spiritual counsels along the way. Yet since the emergence of the Enlightenment in the 18th century, society has generally embraced an inherent belief in the abilities of human beings to chart their own course without need for the Divine. This remains prevalent today and serves as the most significant on-ramp to the wide road leading to destruction.

Prioritizing Our Time

Listening to the opening Gospel for this conference, we would likely conclude that if Jesus invited us to his kingdom, we would never reject the invitation. Yet going back to our two opening questions—what do we truly desire in life and how important is our faith—are we rejecting the invitation of Jesus, perhaps without even realizing it? What excuses do we make? Consider the following story:

> Satan called a worldwide convention. In his opening address to his demons, he said, "We can't keep the Christians from going to church. We can't keep them from reading their Bibles and knowing the truth. We can't even keep them from biblical values. But we can do something else. We can keep them from forming an intimate, continual experience with Christ.

---

88   Cf. *Saint Gregory Palamas: The Homilies*, 15. Homily Three, no. 1.

"If they gain that connection with Jesus, our power over them is broken. So let them go to church, let them have their Christian lifestyles, but steal their time so they can't gain that experience with Jesus Christ.

"This is what I want you to do. Distract them from gaining hold of their Savior and maintaining that vital connection throughout their day.'

"How shall we do this?" asked his demons.

"Keep them busy with the nonessentials of life and invest unnumbered schemes to occupy their minds," he answered. "Tempt them to spend, spend, spend, then borrow, borrow, borrow. Convince them to work six or seven days a week, 10-12 hours a day, so they can afford their lifestyles. Keep them from spending time with their children. As their families fragment, soon their homes will offer no escape from the pressures of work.

"Overstimulate their minds so they cannot hear that still small voice. Entice them to play the radio or CD player wherever they drive, to keep the TV, the DVD player, and their CDs going constantly in their homes. Fill their coffee tables with magazines and newspapers. Pound their minds with news 24 hours a day. Invade their driving moments with billboards. Flood their mailboxes and e-mail with junk, sweepstakes, and every kind of newsletter and promotion.

"Even in their recreation, let them be excessive. Have them return from their holidays exhausted, disquieted, and unprepared for the coming week. And when they gather for spiritual fellowship, involve them in gossip and small talk so they leave with souls unfulfilled.

"Let them be involved in evangelism. But crowd their lives with so many good causes that they have no time to seek power from Christ. Soon they will be working in their own strength, sacrificing their health, and family unity for the good of the cause."

It was quite a convention. And the demons went eagerly to their assignments.[89]

We likely squander time without even realizing it, cramming in so many non-essentials that we have no time for Jesus. Do we put God on hold, thinking he will understand? What are our priorities? What excuses do we make?

The Unprepared Soul

Woe to the soul that does not possess Christ! St. John of Kronstadt wrote:

Those who have not found Christ live in this life without heartfelt faith; they think and care more about worldly things—how to enjoy themselves, now to eat and drink pleasurably, how to dress exquisitely, how to satisfy their carnal desires, how to kill time, because they do not know what to do with it, even though time seeks them and, not finding them, quickly flies away before their eyes. Day after day speeds ahead, night after night, month after month, year after year, until, finally, the last terrible hour strikes, and they

---

89 Geraldine Harris and Kristen Maddox, "Satan's Agenda," posted by Navigators in Christian Living (February 12, 2005). www.navigators.org.

> hear a voice, 'Stop, the course is finished; your time
> has been lost; your sins and iniquities have proceeded
> you; they will fall upon you with all their power, and
> will crush you with their weight eternally.'[90]

There is no time to squander. We need to perform spiritual works while it is still day.[91] St. Paisius Velichkovsky asked, "Why do you not struggle? Why do you waste the time of your life in tumult and vanity?"[92]

St. Augustine admitted that as a young man, he first wanted to sow his wild oats. In his *Confessions*, he wrote:

> But I was an unhappy young man, wretched as at
> the beginning of my adolescence when I prayed for
> chastity and said: 'Grant me chastity and continence,
> but not yet.' I was afraid you (God) might hear my
> prayer quickly, and that you might too rapidly heal me
> of the disease of lust which I preferred to satisfy rather
> than suppress.[93]

Because we do not know the day nor hour when we will make our account before the fearsome judgment seat, we cannot postpone the invitation of Jesus and the abundance he wishes to give us. St. Ignatius Brianchaninov warns, "He who sins willfully and intentionally, hoping to repent later, insidiously schemes against God. He will be struck down by unexpected death, without the time he counted on to begin a life of virtue."[94] He adds:

---

90 St. John of Kronstadt, *My Life in Christ*, Part 1, 205.
91 Cf. John 9:4. "We have to do the works of the one who sent me while it is day. Night is coming when no one can work."
92 St. Paisius Velichkovsky, "Field Flowers," in *Little Russian Philokalia*, vol. 4 (Platina, CA: St. Herman of Alaska Brotherhood, 1994), 68.
93 St. Augustine, *Confessions*, 145.
94 Brianchaninov, *The Field*, 172.

God sees your sins; he patiently bears the sins you commit under his very gaze, this chain of sins that constitutes your life. He awaits your repentance, and at the same time offers salvation or perdition to your free will and choice. And this is the goodness and long suffering of God that you abuse! You do not improve! Your laziness only becomes stronger! You only care for increasing your sins; you only add more and more sins to your previous ones![95]

Do we postpone our salvation? Do we have an excuse for not immediately accepting God's invitation? Will we find ourselves left out in the cold?

Remembrance of Death

We are not kings of the world, nor are we masters of our destiny. Jesus is our king, and we are his disciples; he orders all things and guides us to the abundant life. In turn, we choose whether to accept his offer of salvation. Many Holy Fathers consider the remembrance of death and our mortality as a spiritual work that should lead us to repentance and course corrections during this intermediate stage of the journey, thus preparing us to achieve our true goal. We should shed tears and mourn our sins, freeing ourselves from attachments, both material and emotional bonds.[96] We should avoid sin, maintain our struggle against the passions, cultivate the virtues, and deepen our prayer, always casting our wretchedness before the Lord. We should be anxious to meet him, looking forward to the day of his coming. Archimandrite Zacharias of Essex adds, "Remembrance of death is

---

95 Ibid., 173.
96 Emotional bonds include resentment, bitterness, a desire for justice, or inability to forgive, as a few examples. These are shackles similar to material attachments that prevent us from entering more deeply into relationship with Jesus. That is why Jesus taught us that we must forgive our brother from our hearts. Cf. Matt. 18:35. We must free ourselves from emotional bonds.

extremely beneficial in that it makes man aware of his absolute need for salvation."[97]

At one point, we will stand before the fearsome judgment seat of Christ. Are we ready to render an account? Have our lives merited the promised life in the world to come? Jesus warns us that we must be prepared. He tells his disciples, "Stay awake!" Elder Joseph the Hesychast wrote:

> Death is lurking somewhere, waiting for us, too. Some day or night will be the last one of our life. Wherefore, blessed is he who remembers his death day and night and prepares himself to meet it. For it has a habit of coming joyfully to those who wait for it, but it arrives unexpectedly, bitterly, and harshly for those who do not expect it.[98]

Do not be deceived! There will be a judgment at the end of our earthy life, where all will be deemed worthy of eternal blessedness or eternal punishment based on how they lived this life. This is clearly described in the teachings of Jesus, including the Judgment of Nations,[99] the Parable of the Rich Man and Lazarus,[100] and the Parable of the Talents[101] wherein the lazy servant was condemned for squandering what was given him. Jesus said he had come to create division on the earth. The first words of his ministry were, "Repent, for the kingdom of heaven is at hand."[102] Repentance is a message central to the teachings of the Holy Fathers, who advise repenting immediately to avoid the risk of eternal punishment. Any effort to change these teachings is a distortion of the truth. If we do not accept

---

97 Cf. Archimandrite Zacharias, *The Hidden Man of the Heart*, 22.
98 Elder Joseph the Hesychast, *Monastic Wisdom* (Florence, AZ: St. Anthony's Greek Orthodox Monastery, 1998), 250.
99 Matt. 25:31-46.
100 Luke 16:19-31.
101 Matt. 25:14-30
102 Matt. 4:17.

the invitation of Christ, we will have no share in the heavenly banquet. If we delay acceptance, we are at risk of losing the kingdom. Material attachments and emotional bonds will enslave us. Worldly pursuits will distract us. We risk Jesus saying to us, "I never knew you. Depart from me, you evildoers."[103]

Further, we need to consider a right-ordered relationship with our Creator. Fear of God is not based on fear of punishment.[104] Rather, it is our fear of being separated from him for eternity; Jesus assured his disciples, "I will not leave you orphans."[105] Accordingly, we do not turn away from the false voices of the secular world and our sinful ways because we fear punishment. Instead, we learn to listen to Jesus and flee our sinfulness, which prevents us from being in a relationship with God and accepting his plan for our salvation.

Some would have us believe that there will be a universal restoration in which all (including the Devil) will be saved. This doctrine, called *apokatastasis*, began with Origen and was condemned in 543 by local Church councils and, again, at the Fifth Ecumenical Council (Second Council of Constantinople) in 553. This doctrine is considered heretical because it denies an eternal hell. To be clear, yes, God *offers* salvation to all; however, he does not simply give eternal blessedness to all on a silver platter, any more than pearls are thrown before swine.[106] His gift is far too precious to be squandered or taken for granted. We must provide the effort, desiring God with all our heart, and he will provide the strength we need. St. Paisius

---

103 Matt. 7:23.
104 See St. Theodoros the Great Ascetic, "A Century of Spiritual Texts," *The Philokalia: The Complete Text*, vol. 2, trans. G.E.H. Palmer, P. Sherrard, and K. Ware (London: Faber & Faber, 1981), 36. "By fear he means not the initial fear of punishment, but the perfect and perfecting fear, which we ought to have out of love for him who has given the commandments. For if we refrain from sin merely out of fear of punishment, it is quite clear that, unless punishment had awaited us, we should have done things deserving punishment. But if we abstain from evil actions not through threat of punishment, but because we hate such actions, then it is from love of the Master that we practice the virtues, fearful lest we should fall away from him."
105 John 14:18.
106 Cf. Matt. 7:6.

Velichkovsky suggested, "Wherefore let us love the narrow and difficult path of the sorrowful life, for this narrow and sorrowful path leads to the Kingdom of Heaven."[107]

Reflection

Jacques Fesch led the life of a proverbial loser. He had an abusive father, his parents divorced, and he lost his Catholic faith by age 17. He was lazy, expelled from school due to misconduct, married his pregnant girlfriend in a civil ceremony, then neglected his wife and daughter. He failed in job after job arranged for by his father, failed at business, gave into carousing, and fathered another daughter with a mistress. Overwhelmed and wanting to escape his miserable life, he fixated on obtaining a sailboat to travel to Tahiti. His father would not pay for such an irrational venture, so Fesch unsuccessfully tried to rob a currency changer. When cornered during his escape, he accidently fired several rounds from his revolver. A French police officer died instantly, and three others, including Fesch, were wounded. At his trial, he was condemned to death by guillotine. An atheist when arrested, he spent three and half years in prison. With the help of a prison chaplain, his lawyer who was a devout Catholic, and a monk who was a friend of his wife, a remarkable change occurred: Fesch rediscovered his faith. The letters he wrote from prison are a testimony to his profound conversion from sinner to saint. His cause for canonization formally opened in 1993, and he was given the title "Servant of God." To the monk, Fr. Thomas, he wrote the following in his last letter:

Dear loved little brother,

When you read this letter I shall be in heaven and I shall see Jesus. Before this, of course, the grain of wheat must be ground in the night, and in peace, for

---

107 Velichkovsky, "Field Flowers," 108.

the powers of darkness to be unleashed against me, to kill me … As a light breeze carries off a spring flower, so the divine Gardener will come to pluck my soul and bear it off to Paradise.

Be sure of this, little brother, it takes more than a few hours of struggle before one learns what love is! I have my eyes fixed on the crucifix, and never take them off the wounds of my Savior. I never get tired of repeating, 'It is for you.' I want to keep this image before me to the end, I who will be suffering so little. He suffered so much for me—he, for me—and in his goodness he takes away so many of my sufferings that there is very little left for me to endure.

Dearly loved little brother, I await in dark and in peace. I await love! To being inundated with torrents of delight, and to singing the eternal praises of the glory of the Risen One … God is love!

Have no fear, little brother, I am taking your name to heaven, etched in my heart, and if in the blessed eternity Jesus allows me to speak with him, I shall ask him to bless you and yours and all those whom you care for with tender solicitude. Jesus, in his divine providence, gave you to me as an older brother to watch out for the weaker, younger one. Now, it is I who will be given to you so that you many receive from heaven all the gifts God has showered on me through your prayers, and much more, since I will be at the source of mercy!

Go in peace, little brother. May your road be straight and simple, and one day lead you to where you, too, will rejoin our one Love with the good thief on the cross, who heard that day, 'Amen, I say to you, this day you will be with me in Paradise.'

Until we meet in God, I leave you little brother. If you can, watch over my dear ones, and don't let them ever forget my little girl belongs to the Blessed Virgin Mary! May joy fill your heart and may our Lord Jesus Christ, Father of all blessings, bless and keep you. I embrace you in Christ and Mary.

Your brother in God, Jacques.[108]

Jacques had a firm conviction that he would enter into Paradise. A few days before his execution, he wrote, "No harm shall come to me, and I shall be carried straight to paradise with all the gentleness bestowed upon a newborn child."[109] Are we prepared with similar certitude for the end of our earthly life?

Note that Fesch's conversion was not immediate. When he was first imprisoned, he sent the prison chaplain away. But the chaplain did not give up, and during the first year, Jacques rediscovered his faith, becoming a devout Catholic and bitterly regretting his crime. Despite his lawyer's efforts to appeal his sentence, he accepted his fate, somehow knowing the outcome, yet also certain of his salvation. He wrote letters, kept a spiritual journal, and reconciled with his wife the night before his execution. The prison chaplain attested to the fact that Fesch's faith was not a kind of autosuggestion (hypnotic or subconscious adoption of an idea): It was a grace coming from God, the grace of encounter granted to him in the solitude in his cell. He wrote:

And then, at the end of my first year in prison,

---

108 Lemonnier, 105-6, 109.
109 Ibid., 100.

a powerful wave of emotion swept over me, causing deep and brutal suffering. Within the space of a few hours, I came into possession of faith, with absolute certainty. I believed, and I could no longer understand how I had ever had not believed. Grace had come to me. A great joy flooded my soul, and above all a deep peace. In a few instants everything had become clear. It was a very strong, sensible joy that I felt. I tend now to try, perhaps excessively, to recapture it: actually, the essential thing is not emotion, but faith.[110]

Reflection Questions

1. What pursuits consume my time? What is first? Second?

2. Do I find myself postponing my relationship with God? What is preventing me from having a deeper relationship with him?

3. If I were called right now, would I be prepared to render an account before the fearsome judgment seat of Christ? Why or why not?

---

110 Ibid., 27.

Icon of the Parable of the Great Feast

What excuses will we make to decline the invitation?

Cheese-Fare Sunday: Aposticha Doxastikon

On Cheese-fare Sunday, the day before the start of the Great Fast (Lent), the Church commemorates the expulsion of Adam and Eve from Paradise. Consider the words of the Aposticha, a hymn sung during vespers:

> Adam was banished from Paradise because of the forbidden fruit. He sat before the gates, sighing and lamenting: "Alas! Woe is me! What is happening to me? I have transgressed the commandment of the Lord, and am now deprived of every blessing. O Paradise so

delightful, you were planted for me; and now you are closed because of Eve. Beseech your Creator who has also fashioned me to fill me with the fragrance of your flowers once again."

And the Savior said to him: "I do not desire the destruction of my creation; I wish it rather, to be saved and come to the knowledge of truth; for I do not reject those who come to me."[111]

While our personal choices separate us from God and deprive us of Paradise, it is important to realize that God does not desire the death of the sinner; rather, God wants him to be converted and live.[112] Through his Incarnate Son Jesus Christ, God invites us to return to him. It is up to each of us to accept this invitation, this offer of salvation, which is a segue to our final conference.

---

111 Ruthenian Byzantine Catholic translation. See Metropolitan Cantor Institute, Liturgical Calendar, Cheesefare Sunday, Vespers, 6-7. www.mci.archpitt.org.

112 Cf. Ezek. 33:11. "I take no pleasure in the death of the wicked, but rather that they turn from their ways and live. Turn, turn from your evil ways! Why should you die, house of Israel?"

Accepting the Invitation

"Do not love the world or the things of the world. If anyone
loves the world, the love of the Father is not in him."
(1 John 2:15)

"Do not have Jesus Christ on your lips and the world in your hearts." [113]
(St. Ignatius of Antioch)

Opening Thought

Each of us is called to a life of holiness. God desires salvation and the abundant life for each person. We initially addressed repentance as a foundational theme in the intermediate stage of the spiritual journey described by St. Gregory Palamas. However, this is only part of the equation. In this conference, we will address our call to discipleship—the invitation of Jesus to follow him unconditionally to the Father.

Opening Gospel Reading: The Call of Matthew

Matt. 9:9-13

> A reading from the Holy Gospel according to St. Matthew.

> As Jesus passed on from there, he saw a man named Matthew sitting at the customs post. He said to him, "Follow me." And he got up and followed him.

---

113 St. Ignatius of Antioch, "Letter to the Romans," *The Liturgy of the Hours*, vol. 3 (New York, NY: Catholic Book Publishing Co., 1975), 329.

> While he was at table in his house, many tax collectors
> and sinners came and sat with Jesus and his disciples.
> The Pharisees saw this and said to his disciples, "Why
> does your teacher eat with tax collectors and sinners?"
> He heard this and said, "Those who are well do not
> need a physician, but the sick do. Go and learn the
> meaning of the words, 'I desire mercy, not sacrifice.' I
> did not come to call the righteous but sinners."

> The Gospel of the Lord.

Following Jesus

God calls each of us, and his offer of salvation is completely
gratuitous, reflective of his overflowing love. Jesus is God's personalized
invitation to us to enter into a relationship with him; he knocks at
the door of our hearts[114] and "will not rest until he has moved us
from the gutter to the Palace."[115] To be clear, Jesus did not simply call
the perfect or self-righteous—he came to seek the salvation of all,
including sinners. He calls each of us, and our response should be
akin to Matthew: "He got up and followed him."

An authentic Christian disciple knows Jesus, believes in him, is on
fire with love for him, and follows him with an undivided heart. Does
this describe us, or do we find ourselves increasingly swept away
by the spirit of the age? Is our faith lukewarm? We have discussed
the only way to eternal life: "enter through the narrow gate." Today,
we can observe many responses to the invitation of Jesus from the
qualified response: "Yes, but ...." to attempts to redefine the way,
somehow trying to widen the narrow gate or find a different way.
Matthew got up and unconditionally followed Jesus. And so must we.

---

114 See Rev. 3:20. See also John 15:23.
115 Anthony M. Coniaris, *Tools for Theosis: Becoming God-like in Christ* (Minneapolis: Light
& Life Publishing Company, 2014), 80.

St. Theophan the Recluse wrote:

> A true witness of Christian life is the fire of active zeal
> for the pleasing of God. Now the question arises,
> how is this fire ignited? Who produces it? Such zeal
> is produced by the action of grace. However, it does
> not occur without the participation of our free will.[116]

In the call of Matthew, Jesus's invitation was the grace; however, Matthew consented to this invitation by immediately getting up. St. Theophan explains:

> The divine life is aroused when the Spirit of God
> penetrates into the heart and places there the
> beginning of life according to the Spirit, and cleanses
> and gathers into one the darkened and broken features
> of the image of God. A desire and free seeking are
> aroused (by an action from without); then grace
> descends (through the Holy Mysteries) and, uniting
> with our freedom, produces a mighty zeal.[117]

St. Theophan is clear that zeal is produced through human-divine collaboration: grace provided by God penetrates the heart and is coupled with our free-will choice to respond. He also warns us that we cannot achieve such zeal on our own:

> But let no one think that he himself can give birth to
> such a power of life; one must pray for this and be
> ready to receive it. The fire of zeal with power—this
> is the grace of the Lord. The Spirit of God, descending
> into the heart, begins to act in it with a zeal that is
> both devouring and all-active.[118]

---

116 St. Theophan the Recluse, *The Path to Salvation: A Concise Outline of Christian Ascesis*, trans. Seraphim Rose (Stafford, AZ: St. Paisius Monastery), 27.

117 Ibid., 27-8.

118 Ibid., 28.

The Narrow Gate

This describes a life lived with God, for such zeal and power cannot be achieved without him. Therefore, we must ultimately make the decision: with or without God. We cannot straddle between the two.[119]

This love for Jesus extends to love for neighbor—loving those whom Jesus loves, which means everyone, unconditionally. This is how we find interior peace, that which Jesus desires to give us and which we will never find in the world.[120] Further, Elder Thaddeus of Vitovnica said:

> If our thoughts are kind, peaceful, and quiet, turned
> only toward good, then we also influence ourselves
> and radiate peace all around us—in our family, in the
> whole country, everywhere.[121]

These teachings stand in stark contrast to the secular world where individualism—*me, me, me, I myself*—run rampant. Given attempts to dilute Gospel teachings, our first decision is to determine which Jesus we will follow:

Biblical Jesus	Modern Jesus
Narrow Gate	*Wide Road*
The Way of the Cross	*Spirit of the Age*
Interior Stillness and Harmony	*Turbulent Whirlpool*
True Freedom	*Enslavement to Sin*
Eternal Life	*Destruction; Eternal Damnation*
Preaches God's righteousness	Preaches only love

---

119 See 1 Kings 18:21. "Elijah approached all the people and said, 'How long will you straddle the issue? If the Lord is God, follow him; if Baal, follow him.' But the people did not answer him."
120 See John 14:27. "Peace I leave with you; my peace I give to you. Not as the world gives do I give it to you. Do not let your hearts be troubled or afraid."
121 *Our Thoughts Determine Our Lives*, 63.

Gives salvation, hope, and peace and joy	Gives health and wealth
Warns of sin, judgment, and hell	Never says anything negative
Hated and despised by the world	Loved and accepted by the world
Exalts God, the Father's will	Serves your will, not God's will
Offends the world with the truth	Hates to offend you or others

As written in the Letter to the Hebrews: "Jesus Christ is the same yesterday, today, and forever. Do not be carried away by all kinds of strange teaching."[122] Today, we are faced with many distortions and attempts to "modernize" Christian teaching by being more inclusive, politically correct, less restrictive, more liberated, or more appealing to mass media. "Every type of perversion and depravity has become someone's personal preference and right"[123] and many want a Christianity that will endorse such immoral behavior. Many flock to a gospel of prosperity that certain televangelists have popularized, which is far more attractive than the need for a cross or self-denial.[124]

Yet, Jesus is not trying to fulfill a quota; he wants to save the courageous few who are willing to deny themselves, take up their crosses daily, and follow him.[125] Salvation is open to all, and God desires that all be saved. This is the Good News of the Gospel and our source of hope. However, there are conditions that Jesus set forth: we need to enter through the narrow gate; we need to make a free-will decision to accept the offer of salvation—on God's terms, not our own. We do not dictate the terms. We must repent and believe in the

---

122 Heb. 13:8-9.
123 Matthew Kelly, *Life is Messy* (North Palm Beach, FL: Blue Sparrow, 2021), 39.
124 The prosperity gospel of the modern age is comparable to the teachings of the scribes and Pharisees at the time of Jesus. They believed health, wealth, and prestige were rewards for virtuous living whereas illness, poverty, and various social stigmas were seen as retribution by God for a sinful life. Indicative of this belief, consider the man born blind, John 9:1-41. The disciples asked Jesus, "Rabbi, who sinned, this man or his parents, that he was born blind?" (John 9:2).
125 Cf. Luke 9:23.

Gospel[126]—the Gospel as presented by Jesus and not distorted by the spirit of the age.

No Salvation without the Cross

Today, people would prefer salvation without the cross or a Christianity without struggles. However, such a thing is not possible. St. Ignatius Brianchaninov wrote:

> A Christian who wants to follow our Lord Jesus Christ and to become a son of God by grace, reborn of the Spirit, first must make it a rule to always patiently bear all sorrows—bodily pain, insults from people, attacks from the demons, and the arousal of one's passions. The Christian who desires to please God more than anything else needs patience and a firm reliance on God.[127]

German Pastor Dietrich Bonhoeffer captures well the difference between false and authentic Christianity in his description of cheap versus costly grace. He writes:

> Cheap grace is the preaching of forgiveness without repentance, baptism without church discipline, Communion without confession, absolution without personal confession. Cheap grace is grace without discipleship, grace without the cross, grace without Jesus Christ, living and incarnate.[128]

This is the way the world tries to mold Christianity, to accommodate the spirit of the age, trying to widen the narrow gate, and eliminate

---

126 Cf. Mark 1:15.
127 Brianchaninov, *The Field*, 287.
128 Dietrich Bonhoeffer, *The Cost of Discipleship* (New York: Simon & Schuster, 1995), 44-5.

the Cross. Thus, it tries to devalue the importance of the Gospel of Jesus Christ. To this, Bonhoeffer provides the contrast:

> Costly grace is the gospel which must be *sought* again and again, the gift which must be *asked for*, the door at which a man must *knock*. Such grace is *costly* because it causes us to follow, and it is *grace* because it calls us to follow *Jesus Christ*. It is costly because it costs a man his life, and it is grace because it gives a man the only true life. It is costly because it condemns sin, and grace because it justifies the sinner. Above all, it is *costly* because it cost God the life of his Son.[129]

Our response to the invitation of Jesus is left to us. He desires a free-will choice to follow him under the terms and conditions set forth through his teachings and example. Thus, we are left with the decision. Assuming we will respond to the call, consider the journey to eternal life: As St. Gregory Palamas noted, repentance is a key component of the intermediate stage of our journey, which includes vital spiritual disciplines such as prayer and the sacramental life of the Church.

Accomplishing goals does not happen without planning and effort. For example, if we want to improve our physical health, we might select a diet and exercise regimen. It is a commitment to which we hold ourselves accountable and gauge progress. Similarly, a runner takes a prescriptive approach to pre-race day preparations: drinking a sufficient amount of water, eating the proper foods, and getting enough sleep the night before. All are done to achieve optimal performance during the race.

The spiritual life, too, has an established goal, heaven. To this end, each of us should adopt a "Rule for Life" that allows us to transition through the intermediate stage and grow our relationship

---

129 Ibid., 45.

with God, strive for inner stillness, and gain eternal life. Consider again, the runner preparing for a weekend race. If athletes are willing to exercise these types of disciplines to attain a perishable crown, what are willing to do for an imperishable one?[130] Here are some thoughts to help customize such a rule:

Rule for Life
Not too easy, not heroic – the royal middle way, as suggested by many Holy Fathers. Each individual should choose specific actions best adapted to his or her needs.

Prayer
- Morning Prayer
- Evening Prayer
- Prayer before all meals
- Jesus Prayer
- Silent contemplation

Fasting and Abstinence
- Friday? Abstinence and/or fasting? What is the rigor of the fast (e.g., slice of bread and water, one simple meal)?
- Wednesday? Abstinence? Fasting? Rigor of the fast?
- Determine rigor of fasting during the four fasting periods, most specifically the Nativity Fast and the Great Fast (Lent).

Almsgiving
- Deeds that can reflect love of neighbor. Consider specific actions or deeds: feeding the hungry, visiting the sick or homebound, visiting the imprisoned.
- Commitment to random acts of kindness.
- Involvement in specific parish activities such as feeding the hungry, clothing the naked, visiting those in hospitals or prison, etc.

---

130 Cf. 1 Cor. 9:25.

Repentance
- Daily examination. Confession of thoughts? Confession of thoughts to another?
- Choose a father-confessor.
- Sacramental Confession. Frequency?
- Meeting with Spiritual Father (if available). Frequency?

Sacramental Life of the Church: Holy Eucharist
- Divine Liturgy on Sunday and Holy Days
- Incremental liturgies during the week. Frequency?

Spiritual Formation
- Reading Sacred Scripture. Frequency and quantity: One chapter of the Gospel per day? Other New Testament books? Liturgical readings for the day?
- Reading the writings of the Holy Fathers. Time set aside. Choose a Father. Try different ones. Find one who speaks to me. Read and learn more about that particular Father; consider him a spiritual guide.
- Participation-in-formation programs: The Art of Spiritual Life, Philokalia Ministries (podcasts), etc.

Obedience/Living in Community
- Specific tasks to benefit the household in which the Jesus Prayer could be said: ironing, laundry, mowing the lawn. Instead of listening to music or watching television, do some manual work assisted by prayer.
- Determine other types of fasting: Abstain from social media, television, certain entertainment.

Gratitude – Cultivate a Grateful Heart
- Give daily thanks to God for the blessings and crosses.
- Evening reflection of all blessings received. They often could be missed if one fails to reflect on the day.

Each person should have a unique rule and gradually do more to grow their relationship with God. The temptation with any new program is to do everything at once, which becomes overwhelming, and thus, quickly abandoned. The key is to make incremental progress, growing in one or two areas before undertaking more. This takes us back to the opening conference and the two questions: (1) What do I truly desire? And (2) Is faith important to me? Such a rule establishes priorities and accountabilities, especially if our true desire is eternal life. The objective is to transform our hearts, cultivating a fire within—not just going through motions or following rules merely for the sake of compliance. Simply committing one hour a week to liturgy and five minutes per day for prayer does not leave us in a good position to resist the enticements of the secular world.[131] We need greater balance and firmer ground beneath our feet to repel the assaults of the Evil One.

Authentic Christian discipleship is an "all-in" proposition, not something we dabble in. We should not select sacred practices as simply customs from our heritage. Jesus reminds us to love God with our whole heart, not a divided one. It is not for those seeking the popular, fashionable, or trendy. Nor is it for the hesitant or skittish or those who want to skim the surface—a complete waste of time. However, enduring interior and exterior struggles through suffering and perseverance brings a promise of eternal life backed by Jesus's death on the cross. Crucifixion precedes Resurrection. As one spiritual father said, every fiber of our being must be crucified, whereby we have completely surrendered ourselves to God's Holy Will. We can hold nothing back. We must seek constant purification and never grow weary or complacent regarding matters of the soul. The demons do not rest, and neither can we. Let no one be deceived! This spiritual warfare never ends. St. Antony of Egypt said, "The proper daily labor for a man is to cast his wretchedness before God and

---

131 Cf. Fr. Miron Kerul-Kmec, Homily, Divine Liturgy, St. Nicholas Byzantine Catholic Church, Barberton, Ohio (Dec. 26, 2021).

reckon on temptation until his last breath."[132] Finally, the reception of Christ himself in the Sacrament of Holy Eucharist after sacramental confession should strengthen our resolve to avoid the occasions of sin.

Reflection

Dorothy Day was a stubborn, headstrong woman who had a deep-seated longing for something more. Her heart was constantly searching. A journalist and social activist, she regularly marched to protest the injustices of her day. She lived a bohemian lifestyle, was an avowed atheist, and had Communist leanings. She drank, partied, became pregnant, and had an illegal abortion, afraid of losing the man who had impregnated her. (He left her, anyway.) In 1917, she was imprisoned in Washington, DC, for participating in a protest rally for the Women's Suffrage Movement. She and her group began a hunger strike. In her autobiography, she wrote:

> I began asking for a Bible the second day I was imprisoned, and by the fourth day it was brought to me. I read it with the sense of coming back to something of my childhood that I had lost. My heart swelled with joy and thankfulness for the Psalms. The man who sang these songs knew sorrow and expected joy.
>
> I clung to the words of comfort in the Bible and as long as the light held out, I read and pondered. Yet all the while I read, my pride was fighting on. I did

132 Quoted by St. Dorotheos of Gaza, *Discourses and Sayings*, 146. Discourse VII: On Self-accusation. See also Sirach 2:1-6. "My child, when you come to serve the Lord, prepare yourself for trials. Be sincere of heart and steadfast, and do not be impetuous in time of adversity. Cling to him, do not leave him, that you may prosper in your last days. Accept whatever happens to you; in periods of humiliation be patient. For in fire gold is tested, and the chosen, in the crucible of humiliation. Trust in God, and he will help you; make your ways straight and hope in him."

not want to go to God in defeat and sorrow. I did not want to depend on Him. I was like the child that wants to walk by itself, I kept brushing away the hand that held me up. I tried to persuade myself that I was reading for literary enjoyment. But the words kept echoing in my heart. I prayed and I did not know that I prayed.[133]

How many times have we found ourselves like Dorothy, brushing away the invitation of Jesus, not wanting to go to him in defeat and sorrow, not wanting to give in to his presence because of stubbornness or hardness of heart? Or deep-seated pride? How often have we found ourselves praying, not knowing that we were praying? How often are shackled by guilt for past sins? How often do we want to dictate our own terms for accepting Jesus's invitation? Dorothy's experience is common. With her story in mind, consider the following passage by Sr. Ruth Burrows, a Carmelite nun from England and a well-known spiritual writer.

If we could start from scratch, with no preconceived notions of the route, and if our hearts were firmly fixed on our journey's end, with Gospel in hand we would have no further need of route marking, no need of signposts. Jesus himself, through his Holy Spirit, would guide our hearts aright. And even now I am convinced that anyone who truly seeks God rather than himself will find him, and this in spite of being directed in wrong paths. The Holy Spirit will lead him, secretly, probably painfully, but most surely.

The trouble is so very few of us really do seek God. We want something for ourselves and this is why we

---

133 Dorothy Day, *The Long Loneliness: The Autobiography of Dorothy Day* (San Francisco, CA: Harper, 1952), 80-1.

are anxious to be told the way. We want the path marked out for us, securely walled in, with not a chance of going astray. We are so anxious for this that we cannot afford to listen to the Lord guiding us from within. If we did listen then we would realize that we were merely going around in circles within the given confines, and that if we would find God, we must venture out into the trackless, unknown wastes. While we are busy circuiting the well-worn track described for us by others, we cannot conceive what it is like outside, or even that there is one. So to some extent signpost must replace signpost. On each signpost one word only will be written, however; the name of Jesus, for he alone is the way; there is no other.[134]

Sr. Ruth makes a key point: we should seek God rather than ourselves. We should have no preconceived notions but simply surrender to Jesus. We have discussed the two ways—one leading to life and the other to death, with God or without; there is no middle way or compromise. "All people are called to holiness, all people are called to an unceasing battle with sin, and all people are called to unseen warfare."[135] That is the reality. We can enter eternal life only through the narrow gate that, as Jesus said, few will find. Sr. Ruth defines faith as "a sustained decision to take God with utter seriousness as the God of my life ... (and) a decision to shift the center of our lives from ourselves to him, to forgo self-interest and to make his interest, his will, our sole concern."[136] Without Jesus as our guide, we will be swept along on the wide road leading to destruction. Without him, we will remain lost. With him, all things are possible.[137]

---

134 Sr. Ruth Burrows, OCD, *To Believe in Jesus* (Mahwah, NJ: Paulist Press, 2010), xii.
135 Archbishop Averky Taushev, *The Struggle for Virtue: Asceticism in a Modern Secular Society*, trans. David James (Jordanville, NY: Holy Trinity Publications, 2014), 115.
136 Sr. Ruth Burrows, OCD, *Essence of Prayer* (Mahwah, NJ: Paulist Press, 2006), 20.
137 Cf. Matt. 19:26.

Dorothy Day finally consented to the call of Jesus, leaving the wide road leading to destruction and converting to the Catholic faith. Not only did she embrace Christ, she chose to follow his call through radical discipleship. She founded, with Peter Maurin, the Catholic Worker Movement, a nonviolent, pacifist movement that to this day combines direct aid for the poor and homeless with nonviolent direct action on their behalf. Her cause for canonization has been opened; she has the title of Servant of God. In her own words, she wrote:

> Always the glimpses of God came most when I was alone. Objectors cannot say that it was fear of loneliness and solitude and pain that made me turn to him. It was in those few years when I was alone and most happy that I found him. I found him at last through joy and thanksgiving, not through sorrow. Yet how can I say that? Better let it be said that I found him through his poor, and in a moment of joy I turned to him.[138]

Reflection Questions

1. Like Dorothy Day, how many times have I brushed away the call of Jesus, not wanting to accept that I truly needed him? Have I felt that call deep within? If so, what has prevented me from entering a deeper relationship with him?

2. Return to the original two questions of the retreat: (1) What do I truly desire in life? (2) Is my faith important to me? Based on our discussions, has anything changed?

3. What parts of the Rule for Life do I follow? Which has the greatest impact on my spiritual growth?

---

138 Dorothy Day, *Selected Writings*, ed. Robert Ellsberg (Maryknoll, NY: Orbis Books, 2010), 6-7.

4. Am I willing to accept the invitation of Jesus to follow him? Am I all-in, or are there other things my heart wishes to pursue?

Additional Information

We highly recommend the Paulist film, *Entertaining Angels: The Dorothy Day Story* (1996), starring Moira Kelly and Martin Sheen. Also insightful is the PBS documentary *Revolution of the Heart: The Dorothy Day Story* (2020). In addition, Dorothy Day was a prolific writer of articles and reflections. She was one of four Americans referenced by Pope Francis as having built a better future and shaped fundamental American values, during his address to a joint session of Congress on September 24, 2015. The other three were Thomas Merton, Abraham Lincoln, and Martin Luther King, Jr. The Pope specifically noted:

> A nation can be considered great when it defends liberty as Lincoln did, when it fosters a culture which enables people to 'dream' of full rights for all their brothers and sisters, as Martin Luther King sought to do; when it strives for justice and the cause of the oppressed, as Dorothy Day did by her tireless work, the fruit of a faith which becomes dialogue and sows peace in the contemplative style of Thomas Merton.[139]

---

139 Sarah Parvini, "Who are the Four Americans Pope Francis Mentioned in Congress?" *Los Angeles Times* online (Feb. 24, 2015).

The Temptation of Christ on the Mountain by Duccio
di Buoninsegna. Copyright The Frick Collection.

*"At this, Jesus said to him, 'Get away, Satan! It is
written: The Lord, your God, shall you worship
and him alone shall you serve.'"*

(Matt. 4:10)

Send the Devil packing! Pope St. Leo the Great reminds us:

Christian, remember your dignity, and now that you
share in God's own nature, do not return by sin to

your former base condition. Bear in mind who is your head and of whose body you are a member. Do not forget that you have been rescued from the power of darkness and brought into the light of God's kingdom.

Through the sacrament of baptism you have become a temple of the Holy Spirit. Do not drive away so great a guest by evil conduct and become again a slave to the Devil, for your liberty was bought by the blood of Christ.[140]

140 Pope St. Leo the Great, "Sermon No. 1 on the Nativity of Our Lord," in *The Liturgy of the Hours*, vol. 1 (New York: Catholic Book Publishing Co., 1975), 405.

Bibliography

Aleksiev, Archimandrite Seraphim. *The Forgotten Medicine: The Mystery of Repentance*. Translated by Ralitsa Doynova. Wildwood, CA: St. Xenia Skete, 2006.

Aquinas, St. Thomas. "Conference," *The Liturgy of the Hours*, vol. 4. 563-4. New York, NY: Catholic Book Publishing Corp., 1975.

Ascetical Homilies of Saint Isaac the Syrian, The. Revised 2nd edition. Boston, MA: Holy Transfiguration Monastery, 2011.

Athanasius of Alexandria, St. "The Life of Antony of Egypt," *The Wisdom of the Desert Fathers and Mothers*. 2-76. Translated by Henry I. Carrigan, Jr. Brewster, MA: Paraclete Press, 2010.

Augustine of Hippo, St. *Confessions*. Translated by Henry Chadwick. New York: Oxford University Press, 1998.

_____. *Confessions*, *The Liturgy of the Hours*, vol. 3. 273-4. New York, NY: Catholic Book Publishing Co., 1975.

Balan, Ioanichie. *Elder Cleopa of Sihastria in the Tradition of St. Paisius Velichkovsky*. Translated by Mother Cassina. Lake George, CO: New Varatec Publishing, 2001.

Bolshakoff, Sergius and M. Basil Pennington, OCSO. *In Search of True Wisdom: Visits to Eastern Spiritual Fathers*. New York, NY: Alba House, 1979.

Bonhoeffer, Dietrich *The Cost of Discipleship*. New York: Simon & Schuster, 1995.

Brianchaninov, St. Ignatius. *The Field: Cultivating Salvation*. Translated by Nicholas Kotar. Jordanville, NY: Holy Trinity Monastery Publications, 2016.

Burrows, Sr. Ruth, OCD. *Essence of Prayer*. Mahwah, NJ: Paulist Press, 2006.

————. *To Believe in Jesus*. Mahwah, NJ: Paulist Press, 2010.

Catholic News Service. "Young Adults Want to be Heard by the Church, Study Finds." *Texas Catholic Herald*, January 23, 2018.

Chetverikov, Fr. Sergius. *Elder Ambrose of Optina*, "The Optina Elders Series," vol. 4. Translated from the Russian. Platina, CA: St. Herman of Alaska Brotherhood, 2009.

Chryssavgis, John. "Introduction," *Abba Isaiah of Scetis: Ascetic Discourses*. Kalamazoo, MI: Cistercian Publications, 2002.

Ciobotea, Patriarch Daniel. "The Unity between Theology and Spirituality," in *Patriarch Daniel: Rebuilding Orthodoxy in Romania*. Edited by Chad Hatfield. Yonkers, NY: St. Vladimir's Seminary Press, 2021.

Climacus, St. John. *The Ladder of Divine Ascent*. Translated by Colm Luibheid and Norman Russell. New York, NY: Paulist Press, 1982.

Coniaris, Anthony M. *Tools for Theosis: Becoming God-like in Christ*. Minneapolis, MN: Light & Life Publishing Company, 2014.

Day, Dorothy. *The Long Loneliness: The Autobiography of Dorothy Day*. San Francisco, CA: Harper, 1952.

Didache: The Teaching of the Twelve Apostles. Translated by R. Joseph Owles. North Charleston, SC: CreateSpace, 2014.

Didache Bible: With Commentaries Based on the Catechism of the Catholic Church. 1st edition. San Francisco, CA: Ignatius Press, 2015.

Dinan, Stephen. "Losing Our Religion: America Becoming 'Pagan' as Christianity Cedes to Culture." *Washington Times*, online, Dec. 30, 2019.

Dorotheos of Gaza, St. *Discourses and Sayings*. Translated by Eric P. Wheeler Kalamazoo, MI: Cistercian Publications, 1977.

Evergetinos: The Complete Text, vol. 1. Translated by Archbishop Chrysostomos and Hieromonk Patapios. Etna, CA: Center for Traditionalist Orthodox Studies, 2008.

Hahn, Scott, and Brandon McGinley. *It is Right and Just: Why The Future of Civilization Depends on True Religion*. Steubenville, OH: Emmaus Road Publishing, 2020.

Harris, Geraldine, and Kristen Maddox. "Satan's Agenda," *Navigators in Christian Living* (February 12, 2005). www.navigators.org.

Hesychios the Priest, St. "On Watchfulness and Holiness," *The Philokalia: The Complete Text*, vol. 1. 162-98. Compiled by St. Nikodimos of the Holy Mountain and St. Makarios of Corinth Translated by G.E.H. Palmer, P. Sherrard, and K. Ware. London: Faber & Faber, 1979.

Ignatius of Antioch, St. "Letter to the Romans," *The Liturgy of the Hours*, vol. 3. 329-30. New York, NY: Catholic Book Publishing Co., 1975.

Isaiah of Scetis, Abba. *Ascetic Discourses*. Translated by John Chryssavgis and Pachomios Penkett. Kalamazoo, MI: Cistercian Publications, 2002.

John of Kronstadt, St. *My Life in Christ*, Part 1 and Part 2. Translated by E. E. Goulaeff. Revised and adapted by Nicholas Kotar. Jordanville, NY: Holy Trinity Monastery, 2015.

_____. *Ten Homilies on the Beatitudes*. Translated by Nadieszda Kizenko-Frugier. Albany, NY: Corner Editions/La Pierre Angulaire, 2003.

Joseph the Hesychast, Elder. *Monastic Wisdom*. Florence, AZ: St. Anthony's Greek Orthodox Monastery, 1998.

Karambelas, Archimandrite Cherubim. *Contemporary Ascetics of Mount Athos*, vol. 1 and vol. 2. Translated from Greek. Platina, CA: St. Herman of Alaska Brotherhood, 2000.

Kelly, Matthew. *Life is Messy*. North Palm Beach, FL: Blue Sparrow, 2021.

Kerul-Kmec, Fr. Miron. Homily, Divine Liturgy. Barberton, OH: St. Nicholas Byzantine Catholic Church (Dec. 26, 2021). http://www.stnickbyz.com.

Lemonnier, Augustin-Michel. *Light Over the Scaffold: Prison Letters of Jacques Fesch* and *Cell 18: Unedited Letters of Jacques Fesch*. Translated by Sr. Mary Thomas Noble, OP. Staten Island, NY: Society of St, Paul, 1996.

Leo the Great, Pope St. "Sermon No. 1 on the Nativity of Our Lord," *The Liturgy of the Hours*, vol. 1. 404-5. New York, NY: Catholic Book Publishing Co., 1975.

Lewis, C. S. *Mere Christianity*. New York: Harper-Collins, 1952.

Macarius the Great, St. "Homily 28" *The Liturgy of the Hours*, vol. 4. 595-6. New York, NY: Catholic Book Publishing Corp., 1975.

Mark the Ascetic, St. "On the Spiritual Law: Two Hundred Texts," *The Philokalia: The Complete Text*, vol. 1. 110-24. Compiled by St. Nikodimos of the Holy Mountain and St. Makarios of Corinth Translated by G.E.H. Palmer, P. Sherrard, and K. Ware. London: Faber & Faber, 1979.

Nikodimos the Hagiorite, St. *Concerning Frequent Communion of the Immaculate Mysteries of Christ*. Translated by George Dokos. Thessaloniki, Greece: Uncut Mountain Press, 2006.

Our Thoughts Determine Our Lives: The Life and Teachings of Elder Thaddeus of Vitovnica. Compiled by St. Herman of Alaska Brotherhood. Translated by Ana Smiljanic. Platina, CA: St. Herman of Alaska Brotherhood, 2017.

Paisios the Athonite, St. "Passions and Virtues," *Spiritual Counsels*, vol. 5. Translated by Peter Chamberas. Edited by Anna Famellos and Eleftheria Kaimakliotis. Souroti, Thessaloniki, Greece: Holy Monastery of Evangelist John the Theologian, 2016.

_____. "Spiritual Struggles," *Spiritual Counsels*, vol. 3. Translated by Peter Chamberas. Edited by Anna Famellos and Andronikos Masters. Souroti, Thessaloniki, Greece: Holy Monastery of Evangelist John the Theologian, 2014.

Parvini, Sarah. "Who are the Four Americans Pope Francis Mentioned in Congress?" *Los Angeles Times*, online, Feb. 24, 2015.

Pseudo-Macarius. *The Fifty Spiritual Homilies and the Great Letter*. Translated by George A. Maloney, SJ. New York, NY: Paulist Press, 1992.

Saint Gregory Palamas: The Homilies. Edited and Translated by Christopher Veniamin. Dalton, PA: Mount Thabor Publishing, 2016.

"St. Paisios the Athonite on Spiritual Warfare," *The Ascetic Experience* online (Sept. 28, 2019). https://www.asceticexperience.com.

Sederholm, Fr. Clement. *Elder Leonid of Optina*, "The Optina Elders Series," vol. 1. Translated from Russian. Platina, CA: St. Herman of Alaska Brotherhood, 2002.

Stakhovich, Nun Maria and Sergius Bolshakoff. *Interior Silence: Elder Michael, The Last Great Mystic of Valaam*. New Valaam Monastery, AK: St. Herman of Alaska Brotherhood, 1992.

Taushev, Archbishop Averky. The *Struggle for Virtue: Asceticism in a Modern Secular Society*. Translated by David James. Jordanville, NY: Holy Trinity Publications, 2014.

Theodoros the Great Ascetic, St. "A Century of Spiritual Texts," *The Philokalia: The Complete Text*, vol. 2. 14-37. Compiled by St. Nikodimos of the Holy Mountain and St. Makarios of Corinth. Translated by G.E.H. Palmer, P. Sherrard, and K. Ware. London: Faber & Faber, 1981.

Theophan the Recluse, St. *The Path to Salvation: A Concise Outline of Christian Ascesis*. Translated by Seraphim Rose. Stafford, AZ: The Holy Monastery of St. Paisius.

_____. *The Spiritual Life: And How to be Attuned to It*. Translated by Alexandra Dockham. Safford, AZ: The Holy Monastery of St. Paisius, 2017.

Trisagion Films. *Remember Me in Your Kingdom: The Life of Abba Moses the Ethiopian*. 2017.

Unseen Warfare: Being the *Spiritual Combat* and *Path to Paradise* of Lorenzo Scupoli. Edited by Nicodemus of the Holy Mountain. Revised by Theophan the Recluse. Translated by E. Kadloubovsky and G. E. H. Palmer. London: Faber and Faber, 1963.

Velichkovsky, St. Paisius. "Field Flowers," *Little Russian Philokalia*, vol. 4. 57-128. Platina, CA: St. Herman of Alaska Brotherhood, 1994.

Zacharou, Archimandrite Zacharias. *The Hidden Man of the Heart (1 Peter 3:4): The Cultivation of the Heart in Orthodox Christian Anthropology*. Edited by Christopher Veniamin. Waymart, PA: Mount Thabor Publishing, 2008.

Zander, Valentine. *St. Seraphim of Sarov*. Translated by Sr. Gabriel Anne SSC. Crestwood, NY: St. Vladimir's Seminary Press, 1975.

Acknowledgments

This retreat was developed at the specific request of Fr. Miron Kerul-Kmec, Jr., to support his outreach to college students at Franciscan University of Steubenville and the universities in the Pittsburgh area. He has witnessed firsthand signs of spiritual hunger and a desire by some to find answers in the Church. These are seedlings of hope in the aftermath of destructive forest fires fueled by secular influences. A comprehensive 2015-2017 study by St. Mary's Press, *Going, Going, Gone: The Dynamics of Disaffiliation in Young Catholics*, provides some perspectives on why young people are leaving the Church in epidemic proportion:

- Disillusionment and frustration that their questions about faith were not answered—nor were they given the opportunity to ask.

- Lack of companionship on the spiritual journey.

- Struggles with difficult issues such as abortion, marriage, or contraception.[141]

Stephen Dinan wrote in the *Washington Times* about the significant rise of the "apathetics"—those who do not attend religious services, do not subscribe to a creed, and are losing familiarity with faith. This group is larger than agnostics and atheists combined—increasing by millions each year. They have increasingly disconnected from their churches and have not come back. They are categorized as "Nones," citing no religious affiliation, and in 2019 became the

---

141 Catholic News Service, "Young Adults Want to be Heard by the Church, Study Finds," *Texas Catholic Herald*, January 23, 2018, 2. Reference is made to the survey contained in Robert J. McCarty and John M. Vitek, *Going, Going, Gone: The Dynamics of Disaffiliation in Young Catholics* (Winona, MN: St. Mary's Press, 2017). This survey was conducted from 2015-2017.

largest demographic in the U.S., composed of 23.1 percent of the population, overtaking Catholics and evangelicals. It is estimated that 40 percent of the age 18-to-22 population fit into this category.[142]

Moreover, this was *before* the COVID-19 pandemic that exacerbated the situation. Since then, we've seen draconian measures such as the closing of churches, increased isolation, and fear displacing hope. In this increasingly chaotic religious climate, clashes between Church teachings and secular culture have grown significantly. "We are at an inflection point,"[143] wrote Dr. Scott Hahn and Brandon McGinley. They observed:

> Despite all the bad news both within the Church and on its peripheries, this is one of the best evangelization opportunities in centuries. So many people are looking for answers to the emptiness they feel as the old concepts and institutions that provided identity and structure fade away and as the new idolatries prove unsatisfying. It is always the right time to assert Christ, but there are times when the culture is more open than others. Despite all the apparent dangers, this is one of those times.[144]

Generally, we find that our young people want to understand prayer and the mystical dimensions of their faith, leading to genuine encounters with Jesus Christ. This spiritual and deeply personal dimension cannot be separated from the Church, which is the repository of faith and facilitates such encounters. Some want to separate this connection, claiming to be "spiritual" but independent of the "institutionalized Church." However, this is a delusion that leads individuals on a fruitless search of their own experiences. It

---

142 See Stephen Dinan, "Losing Our Religion: America Becoming 'Pagan' as Christianity Cedes to Culture, *Washington Times* online (Dec. 30, 2019).
143 Scott Hahn and Brandon McGinley, *It is Right and Just: Why The Future of Civilization Depends on True Religion* (Steubenville, OH: Emmaus Road Publishing, 2020), 134.
144 Ibid.

ignores a 2,000-year Tradition of the men and women who have gone before us, striving to follow the Gospel of Jesus Christ and providing us with meaningful spiritual guidance.

This retreat is focused on enabling people to reexamine their faith, realizing the Church *does* have something relevant to say and remains the source of Truth in a darkened world greatly in need of it.

My interest in working with young people began with the inspiration of one person. I am grateful to Donna Rueby, who years ago envisioned the importance of planting and nurturing the seeds of faith in our high school and college students. Through her Surfside Retreats,[145] she sought to expose them to silence and contemplation, desiring to create a foundation for their college and post-college journey. Her vision and inspiration remain with me, and this work is dedicated to her and others who value creating a foundation of faith in our young people.

Fr. Miron Kerul-Kmec, Sr., too, has been a constant source of inspiration as someone who encourages me on the spiritual journey, recommends spiritual reading, and has a passion for evangelization, specifically helping people rediscover the importance of the interior life. His recommended readings have provided significant source material for my writings and in other works. He, too, advocates the formation of young people at the parish level. His focus on the teachings of the Holy Fathers has manifested itself in impactful homilies; his formation class explores the writings of St. Ignatius Brianchaninov.[146] Thank you for your friendship, support, and encouragement.

Another great influence on our young people is Fr. Mark Goring, CC, and his daily YouTube videos. He has a vibrant youth ministry in his parish, St. Mary's Catholic Church in Ottawa, Ontario, Canada.

---

145 So named because the retreat involved a weekend away at rented houses on Surfside Beach located on the upper Texas Gulf Coast.
146 These are accessible to the public as podcasts. See Podbean, *The Art of Spiritual Life.*

(We met when he was a confessor for our high school youth during one of Donna's Surfside Retreats in January 2013.)

Finally, I would like to thank Ginger and Gina DeFilippo for doing an independent read of this manuscript, providing their commentary and perspectives—and catching the elusive typos. Both are members of Fr. Miron's formation class and Gina represents the young adults to which this work is specifically targeted.

To all the servants of God who influenced this work—Donna, Fr. Miron, Jr., Fr. Miron, Sr., Fr. Mark, and Ginger and Gina and their family—may God grant you many blessed years in peace, health, and happiness. *Mnohaja I blahaja lita.*

Fr. Deacon Edward Kleinguetl

Fr. Deacon Edward Kleinguetl, MASp
January 1, 2022
Feast of Our Holy Father Basil the Great,
    Archbishop of Caesarea in Cappadocia

Other Resources Available

Podcasts – Directed Book Studies/Formation Sessions

Fr. Miron Kerul-Kmec, St. Nicholas Byzantine Catholic Church, Barberton, Ohio, The Art of Spiritual Life
   https://artofspirituallife.podbean.com/

   - St. Ignatius Brianchaninov, *The Field.*
   - Homilies

Fr. David Abernethy, CO, Pittsburgh Oratory, Philokalia Ministries
   https://https://www.thepittsburghoratory.org/philokalia-ministries
   https://philokalia.podbean.com/
   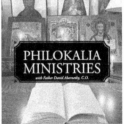
   - St. John Cassian, *The Conferences.*
   - St. John Climacus, *The Ladder.*
   - St. Isaac the Syrian, *The Ascetical Homilies.*
   - St. Theophan the Recluse, *The Spiritual Life.*
   - *The Evergetinos.*
   - *City a Desert.*

Books by This Author

Encounter series

Encounter: Experiencing the Divine Presence. Second Edition. 2022.

Into the Desert: The Wisdom of the Desert Fathers and Mothers. 2019.

The Art of Spiritual Life series

Choosing Life in Christ: A Vocation to Holiness. 2019.

The Fruit of Silence: The Jesus Prayer as a Foundation to the Art of Spiritual Life. 2020.

The Fruit of Prayer: Spiritual Counsels of the Holy Fathers. 2021.

Retreats

Mine Know Me: An Examination of Authentic Christian Discipleship. 2021.

The Narrow Gate: Recalibration on the Spiritual Journey, 2022.

CPSIA information can be obtained
at www.ICGtesting.com
Printed in the USA
BVHW030043150722
642166BV00014B/1510

9 781977 251596